Journal of a Psychoanalysis

Other books by PAUL DIEL

The Psychology of Re-education
The Psychology of Motivation
Fear and Anguish
Psychological Healing
Symbolism in the Bible
Symbolism in the Gospel of John
The God-Symbol
Symbolism in Greek Mythology

Journal of a Psychoanalysis

Paul Diel

Translated from the French
by RICHARD GRAVEL

SHAMBHALA
BOSTON & LONDON
1987

SHAMBHALA PUBLICATIONS, INC.
HORTICULTURAL HALL
300 MASSACHUSETTS AVENUE
BOSTON, MASSACHUSETTS 02115

Library of Congress Cataloging-in-Publication Data
Diel, Paul, 1893–1972.
   Journal of a psychoanalysis.

   Translation of: Journal d'une psychanalyse.
   1. Psychoanalysis—Case studies.   2. Motivation
(Psychology).   I. Title.
RC509.8.D5413   1987   616.89'17   87-9768
ISBN 0-87773-370-8

CONTENTS

«Contents»

Introduction

*T*his personal diary of a psychoanalytic patient illustrates a method of healing which, unlike retrospection and pansexuality, is based on the study of inner motivations. These motivations are given prescientific expressions in various mythologies—the foundations of culture—and in night dreams, but also in psychosomatic symptoms, which are an accurate measure of the degree of aberrance with respect to the meaning of life.

Linguistic wisdom tells us that *inner motives*[1] *are reasons for acting.* While anyone may occasionally act in an unreasonable manner, thereby showing the degree to which he or she is confused by faulty reasoning, that is, wrong motives, the accumulation of thought patterns based on false motives leads to a form of mental illness which manifests as nervous irritability—a psychological state so common as to be considered benign and normal by psychiatrists. However, this nervousness can build up to such an extent that it becomes neurosis, at which point the underlying illogicality of wrong motivations reveals itself through symbolically disguised actions—phobias and obsessions—which can only be overcome by curative treatment. One could then hypothesize that these thought patterns based on wrong

---

[1]The fact that the word *motive* is related to motion and movement, and therefore action, is more obvious in French than in English. (Translator's note)

motives would reach their peak in psychosis, with insanity exploding in the form of deliriums and hallucinations. The fact remains that linguistic wisdom has lumped together under the term *mental illness* these psychopathic states based on underlying distorted motivations. If this term is accurate, it must follow that the aim of any form of curative analysis, that is, mental healing, can only be achieved through the review of false motivations.

A CRUCIAL POINT

While the fundamental question, as stated, may seem to be of purely theoretical import, the hypothesis is undeniably economical. It suggests a natural classification of psychopathic states and their understanding based on one perfectly natural principle: the possibility that human reasoning may go astray.

The diary of a psychoanalysis presented herein relates the ups and downs of the cure; it expresses not only the patient's motives for following the cure, but also his resistances against uncovering his hidden motives. Written by the patient himself, it reveals the secret recesses of his mind.[2] The diarist had no other purpose or theme than to set down in writing the psychoanalytic sessions in order to recall them, thereby improving his understanding. Although the patient was sustained in his endeavor by the positive effects confirmed daily in practical experience, his diary remains nonetheless an exceptional account of an individual's efforts to persevere.

THE ROLE OF WRONG MOTIVATIONS

I should point out that this diary was written some thirty years ago. At the time, adult psychoanalysis was something quite out of the way for me. Working at the Institut de Psychobiologie de l'Enfant, I was primarily in-

[2]The first edition of this book was published in 1964 under the title *Journal d'un psychanalysé* (Journal of a Psychoanalysand).

volved in the rehabilitation of young teenagers, twelve years of age and over. I dealt specifically with cases in which clinical examination had shown that maladjustment was not primarily due to organic disturbances but instead to deficiencies in inner psychological functioning—that is, with emotionally retarded teenagers. From the parents' point of view, emotional retardation almost always gives rise to two highly unwelcome attitudes: disobedience and poor marks at school. In addition, both of these attitudes are expressed through numerous character disturbances, such as apathy, laziness, insolence, and unruliness.

At that point, my research centered on the possibility of reducing the emotional disturbances by putting order into preexisting secret resentments which underlie the behavior and condition the intentions of children whose education has been inadequate.

Both character and behavior are in fact subject to a twofold conditioning: by inner tensions which act as motivating intentions and by environmental excitations. These excitations should be called *action motives*, since they mobilize preexisting inner motivations in view of eliciting a reaction. The linguistic wisdom contained in this term is quite clear: an "excitation" is an incitation to externalize, to act out, and therefore presupposes the existence of an interior mental space.

PSYCHOLOGICAL EXCITABILITY

If this is the case—and it can hardly be denied—it follows that the conditions for mental health and illness cannot be understood by studying only external excitations and excluding internal excitability. Furthermore, it is important to study not only wholesome but also unwholesome feelings—spitefulness, sulkiness, touchiness, one-upmanship, vindictiveness, and the like. The tendency for feelings ("sentiment") to evolve into ill feelings ("resentment") is innate in children and increases with age if the reasoning faculty has been emotionally retarded owing to faulty educational actions on the part of the parents. Nevertheless, since nobody warned the parents of the educational errors to avoid, and since this very omission may quite possibly jeopardize the healthy development of their own reasoning, the blame is not entirely on them. The main fault for which parents can be blamed is not knowing the innermost motivational workings of mind.[3]

Having eluded conscious control, resentment evolves into wrong action motives—wrong because they give rise to wrong attitudes of attack and flight. Thus, resentment is the unsuspected cause of social maladjustment—states of failure or tendencies to triumphant domination, both of which can already be observed in children. In the child (and in the adult he or she will later become), emotional retardation due to distorted motivations based on resentment already determines the overriding features of a nervous personality: excessive irritability and irritating behavior. Both the individual and the people in his or her family and social environment are often driven to nervous irritability or to the very common need to get the upper hand. The result is a mutual provocation that unavoidably affects interactive involvements. Human relations thus become a crucial problem whose solution demands that attention be paid not only to the obvious reciprocity of behavior, but also to unavowed resentments, that is, to wrong motivations.

THE ORIGINS OF THIS DIARY

It has been absolutely necessary to summarize, if only briefly, the main features of a healing method whose application procedures and analytical approach arise, down to their last detail, from practical experience, the central topic of the events written down in this diary.

When I met the anonymous author of this diary, he

---

[3]See P. Diel, *Les principes de l'éducation et de la rééducation*, translated as *The Psychology of Re-education* (Boston: Shambhala Publications, 1987).

was suffering from mental disturbances which manifested as confused, inhibited, and apathetic social behavior. Looking for a way out, he had read the only book I had published at the time, called *Psychologie de la motivation: Théorie et application thérapeutique.*[4] Shortly thereafter, he came to me and requested to be analyzed.

In the attempt to enlarge an experience which had been overly restricted to the rehabilitation of children and adolescents, I had long since broadened my interests to include adults. I therefore agreed to be the analyst of a forty-year-old man who, for many reasons, seemed especially likable.

Our cooperation extended over a period of several years, at the rate of two sessions per week (excepting vacations). During each of these sessions, which lasted approximately two hours, we attempted to unravel the motives which underlay the patient's everyday deficiencies and to interpret his dreams. Unmasking secret motives, condensed by dreams into meaningful images, makes it possible to amplify the theme and explain the general structure of faulty mental functioning, thereby reviewing and finally objectivizing it. The aim is not to make a particular symptom disappear (this is relatively easy), but to cleanse the unhealthy ground of inner deliberations in which wrong attitudes evolve from the pathogenic seeds of material and sexual desires and anxieties, as intensified by the imagination.

The duration of the curative treatment depends on the extent to which the person being analyzed feels it is necessary to deepen the process. The normalization of a child's or an adolescent's behavior can often be achieved in a few months, sometimes even in a few weeks. However, in the case of some adults in whom the distorting habits—the emotional and ideological resistances—are too ingrained, it

---

[4]Translated as *The Psychology of Motivation* (Claremont, Calif.: Hunter House, 1987).

may prove desirable to extend the treatment beyond the period of social normalization. This is especially true if the patient shows an above-normal need for deepening his insight, something which he can only appease by acquiring an independent understanding of the entire process of inner mental functioning. In such a case, the expanded aim of the cure is not only to free the patient from present disturbances, but also to transmit a method of self-control with which he can protect himself from relapses once the work with the therapist is over. In this particular case, the patient had expressed the desire to prolong the analytical process far beyond the point of behavior normalization.

FREEDOM FROM SELF-DECEIT

Approximately one year into the treatment, the patient decided to keep a diary. At that point, the knowledge he had acquired with regard to distorting resentments, along with his resulting capacity for self-control, had condensed sufficiently into what could be termed a center of crystallization. Through the willing cooperation of the patient, this center could be expanded and thus genuinely assimilated. In his diary, the patient reflects on some of the sessions, summarizing and often elaborating them; prompted by the analysis, he tries to face his inner problems as objectively as possible.

To understand these journals, one need not be conversant with the different doctrines and therapeutic techniques of analytic psychology. However, inasmuch as this text is an example of how I have put into practice certain personal notions for which I can assume no familiarity on the part of the reader, I feel it is necessary to highlight the essential difference between the method used herein and mainstream psychoanalytic theories.

Psychopathy tends to be considered a disorder of social behavior. While it is true that adjustment to a social norm is essential for the individual and helps appease inner conflicts, social life and the rules it is played by are often inadequate in terms of the meaning of life. What can the value of a therapy be if it does not offer the patient a sane orientation toward life? Moreover, what can the meaning of life be (in psychological terms) other than to free oneself from the self-deceit of wrong motivations and wrong justifications, which lead in turn to distorted and vitally unhealthy social interactions? Although methodical self-observation is the only way to achieve control of one's inner motives, to have a wholesome effect this process must be the exact opposite of the morbid, egocentric, and self-indulgent introspection all too often encountered. Objectivizing self-control aims precisely at freeing the ego, enabling it thereby to establish healthy social relations, unfettered by either overexcitement or inhibition. Such an expanded approach to the issues of mental health and illness, based on incorporating the individual into the broader framework of life and life's meaning, has innumerable consequences. This cursory statement of my observations is not presented here for polemical purposes; I am not trying to convince the reader, but to orient him by summarizing as briefly as possible the general principles which have governed the writing of this diary.

BLIND EMOTIONALITY VERSUS SELF-ACTUALIZATION

Without explaining in detail the usual investigatory techniques and their reversal into methods of self-observation and self-control, it might be helpful to outline one consequence of this approach which to me seems fundamental. Inasmuch as inner motivations must necessarily be divided into two groups—sane and insane—their study exceeds the strict limits of medical research. Since society itself is quite possibly perverted, the true solution to the problem of leading a healthy life can no longer be seen in terms of social adjustment; therefore, the focal point of the problem shifts. The term *society* is merely an abstraction: only individuals can actually live; while it is true that individuals are co-conditioned by social norms, it was individuals in the first place who, through their interactions and reflections, created these more or less sane or insane norms (traditions, institutions, ideologies). Mental illness can thus no longer be regarded as radically opposed to the norm: all human beings, even those usually considered to be most normal, are affected, in varying degrees of intensity, by this generalized malaise and its root cause: wrong motivations.

Mental illness and the search for its cure thus become the central problem in life, one whose solution can only be found by studying the energy exchange between an individual and society. This exchange is regulated both by the emotionally blind force of sexual and material desires and by the elucidating force of reason. Inasmuch as both desires and reason, as motivating forces, are inner mental phenomena, the problem being studied is purely internal and manifests as an inner conflict between blind emotionality and that part of mind which can estimate the true value of things. Human life is conditioned only accidentally by the stimuli of social relations; it is conditioned in its essence by the different inner motives that all human beings develop deep down inside through their intentions—right or wrong, healthy or unhealthy, sane or insane, avowed or considered unavowable. The analysis of these motivating intentions as a whole is crucial, for inner motivation is the essential principle of self-determination and consequently of responsibility—not so much in terms of society as of each human being's own mastery of self in the face of more or less favorable environmental promptings.

Before reaching their reactive release, right and wrong motives condition in every individual the *inner deliberation* through which sane or insane voluntary decisions are developed. Motives considered unavowable on account of their vital insanity or their social undesirability lead to perverted volitions and to unhealthy actions, which can become heightened to the point of manifesting as psychopathic behavior. At the social level, these interactions based on wrong motivations and vain justifications give rise to mutual resentments: triumphant stances, grudges, excessive hate, self-pity, and so forth—the entire retinue of perverted feelings and distorted character attitudes on which psychopathology is based.

It is this entire tangle of inner resentments that the patient attempts to unravel through writing, in order to make of his diary a tool for curative self-control.

A JOINT EFFORT

At the beginning, far from being in favor of this diary, I actually advised my patient against it. My reluctance came from the fear of seeing the effort degenerate into a self-indulgent display, a danger inherent in every attempt of this nature. Quite possibly, the vanity of talking to oneself about oneself could have prevailed over the will to be objective, with the concurrent risk of giving in to the temptation of fallacious self-justification or excessive self-blame. As time went on, however, judging his endeavor to be a genuine attempt at clarification, I resolved instead to monitor it. Since the patient's self-control must obviously be supervised by the analyst, I decided to deal with the pages that the patient brought to the sessions in the same way I would have done with any other material to be analyzed. The way the patient rephrased in writing both his inner experience and the guiding ideas brought to light in the process had the advantage of disclosing to the analyst, in the clearest possible manner, the degree of understanding achieved. For curative reasons, it proved necessary to revise together all the passages which still contained imprecisions.

This revision in no way jeopardizes the genuineness of this document, for genuineness in a therapeutic situation is based not on pseudo-originality but on an effort toward truthfulness guided by the analysis. The sublimatory experience (character formation) should go hand in hand with a genuine spiritual effort (formulation of guiding ideas). Not only are they both productions of the mind, but they are also the only ones possessing the attribute of genuineness—provided a proper method is used, one which reveals the healthy and unhealthy aspects of mental processes. The passages in the patient's diary containing general reflections are not the result of gratuitous interpretations. On the contrary, they have the import of guiding ideas (i.e., action motives) drawn from the curative experience and help broaden the field of experimentation. With the proliferation of analytic methods nowadays, only one assertion remains unquestionable: no therapeutic process can succeed unless a consensus is reached between patient and analyst. It was to establish this necessary consensus that my patient and I edited together the generalizations which are inevitably included in some of the chapters.

THE DUST OF RESENTMENTS

Further editing proved necessary when, rereading these journals years after they were written, it occurred to me to publish them. The analysis is now over, the patient has been cured; both conviction and consensus have been established. The resistance and hesitation to which this diary bears witness have been overcome. These pages contain, besides the account of the patient's life, the guiding ideas which he gradually made his own. The solemn, sometimes ponderous tone which emerges from the text as a whole is due to the fact that the patient tells only of his conflicts, failures and disappointments. The sense of success and satisfaction, even of joy, which accompanies the progressive dissolution of these negative states is also expressed; however, since the gradual regaining of balance is experienced as joyful feelings free from contradictions which, for this very reason, provide no material for analysis, it would have been superfluous for the patient to dwell on and describe these feelings in detail.

Admittedly, it did not seem to me as I reread these notebooks that the patient had actually recorded all the problems dealt with in the analysis; the aim of a diary is obviously not to present the totality of themes essential to the study of motivations. Nevertheless, as it stands, this diary serves to illustrate the method of analysis used. One minor change aimed at orienting the reader and imparting a certain cohesiveness to the text was to give the chapters titles.

The reader would miss the point of these journals if, instead of considering them as tending only toward truthfulness and simplicity—and therefore as an instructive and moving human document—he should get upset at the slimness of the events recounted or at certain stylistic imperfections. The author has no literary experience and no literary pretensions. His journals are not to be compared with the confessions of great writers. In these artistic productions, which can be real marvels of language, one occasionally comes across introspective inspirations of great value from the point of view of truthfulness. Still, needless to say, their instructive scope is diminished by the absence of a genuine method of elucidation and by the fact that imaginative dramatization delights in narrating above all the great ups and downs of life.

The things that reveal any human being's state of mind most deeply are to be found not in the story of the great moments of that person's life (moments which the nervous individual often resists quite courageously), but in the most trifling incidents of everyday living. It is these apparently insignificant and unimportant details which insidiously trigger off endless indignations and brooding in the hypersensitive nervous person, making him waste his entire life and depleting his energies insanely. It is this essential dissipation which must necessarily be corrected.

This dissipation manifests through the transformation

of every feeling into morbid resentment: imaginary humiliations and victories, feelings of superiority or inferiority, shame at others' opinions, excessive self-justification and self-blame, emotional complaints and vindictive criticism, scrupulous inhibitions and the yearning for shameless disinhibition, etc. This dust of resentments, apparently imponderable, is constantly churned up by moments of morbid introspection, misguided attempts on the part of the subject to put order into his mind which plunge him into a semiconscious dream state.

Corrective analysis and its method of elucidating introspection aim at stopping self-indulgent or anguished daydreaming and achieving a more lucid presence of mind vis-à-vis reality and the self. Far from being a waste of time and energy, introspective analysis, by making the ground of inner deliberations wholesome again, is the only means to gain time and to recover dissipated energy, since it makes both time and energy usable in view of socially significant activity.

THE ESSENTIAL REMEDY

In support of this statement, I will conclude by outlining briefly one of the most important aspects of the study of motives—one which may possibly give the reader a glimpse of the vastness of its scope.

The "ill-bred"—that is, inadequately socialized—child, whether frustrated or spoiled, is living proof that there exists an innate temptation to respond to educational errors with secret false justifications. Once this unhealthy habit has been acquired, it tends to grow continually throughout a person's life. The power of wrong justifications based on imagination is such that these will distort all the data of reality.

When the child becomes an adult, he no longer holds his parents primarily responsible for his anguished, unsatisfied desires—which can now never be satisfied because of their very overemphasis. However, the childishness of his emotional complaints persists, with his claims and demands manifesting in relation to his social situation, be it unfavorable or privileged, and even in relation to life itself, which showers its gifts on some people and cheats others. This transformation of real or imagined injustices into claims and complaints lays the ground for feelings of frustration to arise, even when the subject has all he could wish for at the social level. Feeling frustrated, he will fall prey to vindictiveness for not being the darling child of life.

Whether it is the frustrated child's unfulfilled need for affection and esteem or the spoiled child's nostalgia for affection and overesteem, it is essentially these feelings which survive in the form of motivations based on subconscious memories. (The Freudian school of psychoanalysis uses the label "Oedipus complex" to describe these subconscious memories and the wrong attitudes of attack and defense born from them, but interprets them from a purely sexual point of view.)

Since nobody can be so well favored by life as to be endowed with every possible gift and privilege, emotional complaints will always find a pseudo-justification in some hardship or other. Whether the nervous person is robust or sickly, physically strong or weak, tall or short, good-looking or homely, socially privileged or underprivileged, rich or poor, intelligent or unintelligent, his or her jealousy and emotional complaints will seek consolation in vain triumphs and a bloated sense of self, which will switch over to loss of self-esteem accompanied by a sense of guilt. The source of the dissatisfactions that we consider unbearable and unsurmountable can be found deep within each of us. As long as the nervous individual does not probe his inmost depths in order to dry up the wellspring of vain overestimation of his own self-worth, he will be overwhelmed by feelings of anxious guilt throughout his entire life.

The reversal of the emotional accusation of others into

self-accusation, self-blame, and guilt shows the persistence of the inescapable sense of responsibility, even when repressed by self-justification born of vanity. It is self-justifying repression, more than any other fault, which is the root of the evil; with each real failure, it further reinforces blindness with regard to oneself—mental deficiency—until it finally manifests in the guise of the manifold symptoms of "mental illness."

Since the reversal of just into unjust, sane into insane, is what triggers wrong motivations, even the privilege of intelligence is unable to provide a remedy as long as corrective reasoning refuses to concentrate on observing this central phenomenon. Since every man and woman has the predisposition to generate wrong justifications based on repression, everybody—all of humankind—is subject to the innate temptation to camouflage the essential fault of human nature—that is, motivations based on false justifications —instead of studying the origins and psychopathological consequences of this fault.

The most basic and the most harmful of all the perverted reversals is the tendency to consider only the painful and shameful aspects of acknowledging one's major fault—one's vanity—instead of realizing that the essential remedy for this fault lies in becoming aware of it.

WHY WAS THIS JOURNAL PUBLISHED?

This journal was written only because its author dared to go against the most common prejudice concerning elucidating introspection: he had the actual courage to face himself. It is also due in part to a socially privileged situation which allowed him the leisure of writing.

Quite possibly, some of the readers of this book may themselves fall prey to the reversal described above and, disgruntled, try to transform the merit of having written this diary into blame, claiming that only the patient's well-to-do situation and free time made this attempt at self-elucidation possible. This is one of the reasons for which the author, while agreeing to the publication of his journals, has chosen to remain anonymous. His anonymity in no way denies his pride at having dared write a diary based on the only genuine motive—the search for balance.

Considering that the search for truth, especially the truth about oneself, is a need common to all human beings and one which runs deeper than the need for camouflage, I felt it might be useful to publish this document in spite of its shortcomings. The struggle between these two tendencies is an essential theme of human life and manifests with greater or lesser intensity at the level of each person's inner deliberations. The arena of this struggle is the person's own conscience; its aim is fundamental freedom. In this arena, right and wrong motivations confront each other in a battle whose stakes are a life of satisfaction or dissatisfaction, joy or anxiety—in other words, a life of mental health or imbalance.

Assuming that the science of motivations is sufficiently advanced to allow us to set forth the conditions for gradually making the thinking mind wholesome again, this diary should be considered no more than a reflection and a brief summary of this science in its developmental stage. Nonetheless, by documenting the author's progress, it may help the watchful reader recognize himself and encourage him in the secret battle being waged within his own mind.

Journal of a Psychoanalysis

« I »

Beginning of the Analysis

I can say without exaggerating that, until my encounter with psychology, I had spent my entire life between four walls of anxiety. From my first disappointments as a school-boy unable to live up to his teachers' expectations to my false starts as an adult badly in need of growing up, I have always felt, percolating through my being, the complaint and distress of not being able to meet the demands of an environment whose unsympathetic hostility was no more than the product of the daydreams that shut me off from life. "What am I doing in this world? I feel incapable of anything. All around me people have knowledge; they can act and achieve their goals."

Fortunately, my inheritance has enabled me to delude others. Yet I myself know that if it were not for the privilege of being relatively well-off, life would long since have done me in. "What will happen to me if I ever run out of money? My state of decay will be laid bare for everyone to see." Worries of the well-to-do? Partly, perhaps. Yet the real problem lies elsewhere. After all, some rich people do manage to put their skills to good use; they not only live in external comfort but also achieve a relative peace of mind. And how many poor and underprivileged people, as nervous as I, imagine that the real reason for their dissatisfaction is their lack of material wealth! The trouble is actually far more deep-rooted: it is not in the circumstances but in myself, in each one of us. My riches are obviously an enviable possession. I own them, yet instead of appreciating them as a basis for material security, I turn them into a source of anxiety.

I am obsessively concerned with money. I am overwhelmed with worries. Continually preoccupied with the fear of losing my fortune, I am tormented by the desire to earn money, without knowing how to go about it. Every attempt to invest my money, instead of yielding a profit, has led to losses which have reinforced my apprehensiveness. When I have tried to get around my own incompetence by entrusting my interests to others, in the long run I have always discovered that I was being cheated—such an easy prey was I. So what can I do? How can I act, if I can get neither grip nor foothold on solid ground? I suffer from a weakness of the will that is more dangerous than laziness— this dreadful laziness I have always been accused of for as long as I can remember, ever since my earliest academic failures. It is true that I lack courage—but what could I do even if I did have it, never having specialized in any field of study and totally unfamiliar with the language of business, as obscure to me as Chinese? Even when the facts are explained to me, even when I understand them, I feel totally devoid of any opinion; I feel stupid for lack of any skill. Is it courageous to take on a responsibility in which I have no professional training, knowing in advance that I cannot shoulder it? Only manual or mechanical labor requiring no initiative or special knowledge would be within my capabilities—only occupations devoid of interest or appeal such as laborer or office worker. What a state of moral ruin! Exactly the type of disaster I am afraid of. All I have to do is wait for the fateful day in which I will find myself laying bricks in a strange city. What can I do, since I am unable to wait for this moment without anxiety? Should I freeze, play dead? But I cannot avoid thinking, wishing, spending money as long as I am alive! All these signs of life are inevitably permeated with an anxiety that inhibits me all the more. If only the anxiety were limited to material cares . . . but the inhibition extends to all areas of life.

It is horrifying to feel rejected by life. To live without living, without ever feeling alive, is like being swallowed up by a nightmare.

Expecting nothing more from myself, anguished by my past, present, and future, drifting aimlessly, in my panic I have consulted astrologers and soothsayers, magicians and clairvoyants. I can barely express my feeling of utter helplessness. Every move seems fraught with dangers, every decision impossible; I feel I am walking through an endless night because my maladjusted eyes do not know how to see. Why not play dead once and for all and put an end to this?

But one day somebody started to dispel the darkness, to explain to me the secret causes of my maladjustment; he showed me how to find a remedy, how to see. For the first time in my life, I was not being urged to be any particular way, to do one thing or another; I was not being told that I had to want to get better, that I must shake myself out of it—unfortunately, I am exactly the opposite of what I "should" be, and all the good advice has done nothing by increase my distress. Now, at long last, I was being given reasons for why I was not as I should be. It was the chance of my life. I had encountered psychology in its most unexpected form: it endeavored to detect the inner motives of my weaknesses.

Starting from my everyday behavior, it provided me with a blow-by-blow description of myself, of what it labeled "the nervous personality." I recognized myself immediately, since every feature of this description matched my anxiety—my extraordinary anxiety, my nameless anxiety, an anxiety so incomprehensible as to seem absolutely unique. There it was, laid out for me to see with all its ins and outs, its reasons explained in detail and its unsuspected origins revealed: my vanity. Of course my vanity rebelled and argued back, yet deep within myself I had acknowledged it. "Wanting to be superior to everybody, imagining that to be the case, is the best way to end up not only feeling inferior to everyone but actually being inferior. . . . Come, now, am I not an extremely modest person, after all? My goals are not at all ambitious. All I want is a bit of confidence, of good sense, like everybody else!" Little by little, almost in spite of myself, my awareness began to focus on my underlying daydreams. At that point I started to discover my true ambitions, nourished since my childhood by fictional heroes. The man acclaimed by the crowds, the man who fearlessly braves adversity, the explorer, the war hero—but also the rich mogul traveling with his retinue of lackeys and beautiful women from one luxury hotel and resort to another; the somber, good-looking young man, loyal and sensitive, cruelly wounded by human malice, who will one day be discovered by an angel of goodness; the righter of wrongs, sincere and carefree, courageously punishing villains; the scientist or researcher, humbly devoting his life to a worthy cause. "But I don't want to be all that! It's absurd!" Nonetheless, I had now become aware of identifying so much with my heroes' exploits that my everyday life, the life I led outside this communion, seemed dreary, not worth living, hopeless. "So might not the psychologist be right when he says that the only role I consider worthy of myself is that of the hero? And might it not be true that this form of vanity demands that I place myself above other mortals?"

But more—this superiority has to be acknowledged by others; in actual fact, I need the world's approval. This resembles closely the "anguished comparison with others" which my psychologist claims to be inherent in vanity. Do I not find it incredibly irritating to hear others being praised? I feel entitled to that praise; only I deserve it. I am being robbed of my rightful due; it is being stolen from me and given to others. Or perhaps the praise is really a devious allusion to my inferiority? In fact, I only dream of superiority without ever fulfilling it. The loftier my dreams, the more wretched I actually feel. I feel guilty and devastated at not being able to put my dreams into practice; I wallow in self-pity and blame the world for not understanding me. Does not the sense of superiority/inferiority correspond precisely to these feelings of guilt, sentimentality, and accusation—variations on the theme of vanity?

Vanity claims to unite in a single person every possible form of superiority, be it spiritual, material, or sexual. If I chance to read a short biography of a scientist, I envy the life he must have led—whether he died unknown is of no importance, since his posthumous fame alone is enough to arouse my covetousness. Very quickly, however, his life seems to me to be "lacking in women, leisure, and luxury." In immediate reply to this lack, there arises the image of joyful debauchery, of colorful adventures brimming over with lustful delights and fiery embraces. Yet every time I let myself be swept along by a group of debauchees whose verve succeeds in making me lose my inhibitions, as soon as my lust had been appeased I inevitably feel tainted by an unbearable defilement. All I remember is a disgusting drama played out by pathetic characters. The same thing is true of opium's artificial paradise, which only leaves the dismal memory of a circle of mindless smokers bent over a lamp. As for the young women around whom I used to spin out my marriage fantasies—if a woman was beautiful, she was bound to be too elegant, therefore trivial and unintelligent! If she was not trivial, then she was most likely a boring bluestocking. If she was endowed with all the personal qualities I demanded, then her flaw would be her lowly social status, or else her lack of wealth or titles, which would make her unworthy of my origins. And if she happened to have all these other attributes, I would find her lacking in gentleness and kindness. In actual fact, all this discrediting was a construct of my imagination, aimed at justifying my avoidance of women: I feared that a woman possessing only a fraction of the qualities I demanded could never be interested in a being so absurd and abject. All this might seem ludicrous, even impossible, but it really is what does on inside me and can have no other explanation but my absurd arrogance, my boundless vanity.

Nonetheless, the overall explanation by itself would not have been enough to convince me. It was only as the psychotherapy progressed, as I began to see that all my failings were interrelated and had a coherent texture in spite of their apparent incoherence, that I started to feel my resistance give way. The closer I would get to grasping its structure, the more it would crumble. The individual pattern I saw in myself was only an exaggerated version of the character distortions from which, to a greater or lesser extent, all human beings suffer—although they may seem perfectly adapted to a world in which vanity and its variations are all the more powerful because their grip is not only misunderstood but knowingly denied.

At long last I was beginning to understand. The more insight I acquired into the reasons for my anxieties, failures, and sense of despair, the more the world around me lost its magical hostility. Gradually, the feeling of my own responsibility started to dawn on me and I became aware that the world's hostility toward me was a reaction to my own behavior, that it was up to me to reconcile myself with the world. My entire attitude toward the world had been skewed. I had made one mistake, one vital mistake, and by becoming aware of it I could hope to avoid repeating it. For the first time, hope had found a way into my life.

Hearing my most intimate motivations described with disarming precision and logic, my agonizing feeling of isolation started to vanish. I was entering a community of suffering, made up of countless nervous individuals. Although I was dismayed to find out that I was not the exceptional creature which my imagination had conjured up, the unbearable suffering which comes of feeling excluded from life and condemned to die left me no choice but to begin the curative experience.

« 2 »

Professional Life and Repercussions from My Past

*I*f there has ever been a situation that made me feel acutely uncomfortable, it is my daily work environment at Dictio.

Over a year ago I chanced to meet a businessman named Robert, a person with a delightful, intelligent, and assertive personality. He talked to me with great fervor about a certain appliance he was manufacturing which was as yet not very well known, and painted a glowing picture of my future prospects. He had just broken with his partner and was looking to replace him. I let myself be talked into joining his company and investing a rather large sum of money. Since my financial interest in Dictio was to be much larger than his, we had agreed to share management responsibilities. However, for fear of proving inadequate, I in fact reliquished control to Robert. Although I knew he was a novice at business, it soon turned out that, behind his apparent confidence, he was less experienced than I thought. The normal thing would then have been for us to learn the ropes together. This was not to be: while his self-assurance and intellectual abilities slowly made him bolder and led him to take on ever more authority, I evolved in the opposite direction. Unable to have any clear viewpoints of my own, I ended up submitting completely to his; he had rendered me powerless.

Thus, I feel paralyzed by fear every time I have to assume any kind of responsibility. I ask myself anxiously: "What would Robert do in my place? Would he approve of my initiative? Was I right to do this? Won't I look stupid to him?"

This way of comparing myself in my imagination to an idealized figure who holds the truth prevents me from having any real presence of mind. In our everyday dealings, instead of following his arguments I listen to the whispers of my own inner voices, which never stop commenting on the favorable or unfavorable impression I may be making on him. Only now am I starting to become aware of these whispers, which have no doubt always obsessed me without my ever noticing them consciously. They are probably one of the consequences of the secret imperatives I follow, which compel me to appear exceptional, to always seem better than everybody else since I am quite unable to actually be better.

One of the most common forms that my anxiety takes comes from the paralyzing afterthoughts which pursue me in all my relationships: "What do people think of me? Could my indecision possibly pass unnoticed?" However, in this case, by comparing myself to Robert, my agony is heightened even more: "Of course *he* would know what to do!"

Thus I suffer from feeling inferior, with the result that Robert becomes for me a paragon of competence in contrast to my own incompetence. My wounded self-esteem has given rise to a hostility which is slowly but surely destroying any warmth there might have been in our relationship and may quite possibly lead to a new failure in an undertaking that has barely begun. More than a partner, Robert has become a rival I must overthrow—as well as an example I would like to follow, a person I have such excessive admiration for that I have set him up as a kind of idol beyond my reach in order not to suffer from my vain hopes of equaling him.

Is that all I want, to be his equal? No, I would actually like to supplant him, although I may feel incapable of it! I want to crush him, since his very presence is a constant reminder of my own incapacity. Far from being the real, imperfect human being who lives on this earth, Robert has become, in my mind, an imaginary being, a construct of my fantasy embodying the obsessive fears born of all my past hopes and failures. This mental "Robert" watches and spies on me, and also judges, accuses, and condemns me. He is a concrete symbol of my vanity at its most trivial, on the level of material success. Precisely because he represents the counterimage of my inadequacy, he sparks off my feelings of inadequacy. While it is true that I am incompetent as far as running the business is concerned (all my energy is sucked up by my irritation), this real incompetence is constantly worsened by an inhibiting anxiety based on contrast with the exaggerated competence I project onto Robert. In addition, as I have been able to observe on many occasions, my continually wounded vanity and my arrogant submission trigger off Robert's own triumphant vanity. His vanity makes him attempt to impose his will on me more and more, with the result that, in the long run, he has in actual fact become arrogant and insufferable. If I had all my wits about me instead of living in agony, if my generalized anxiety did not prevent me from having presence of mind, I would shoulder my task to the best of my abilities and not suffer overmuch for my inadequacies. Instead of trying to match someone else's capabilities, I would do what is necessary to develop my own by fighting this obsessive comparison. This seems to be the only way to cope with the situation.

I am far from being good at business; in fact, my entire education has helped push me away from it. However, business for me holds a promise of success and represents proof of social and material effectiveness. Not only is earning money a means to escape from my obsessive worries, but it also represents power, prestige, admiration—if not the artistic glory that I used to dream about in younger days. My real inadequacies make me want to outclass everybody in everything. This inhibiting anxiety is a burden to my business life, all the more since, like everyone else, I admire material success as a decisive proof of strength of character.

The result is that I end up perceiving this incompetence as a congenital defect of vital importance. In public, I often bring up my innate lack of business sense as a way of propping up my self-esteem. This explains my tendency to refer to my aristocratic titles or my artistic temperament, since I can then wax scornful about commercial transactions and cut short others' imagined contempt. Since I do not want people to think that I am blind to my own weaknesses, I make the first move and play the part of the wise man who knows himself, all the while taking care to blame my extravagantly confessed inadequacy on a fate I am not responsible for. I let others think that it would be unfair to accuse me, that it would actually be more appropriate to pity me. However, despite my tendency to bemoan my fate and play the victim, my self-esteem cannot stand commiseration. I avoid this displeasure by suggestively referring to my pedigree: "The virtues of my ancestry are unsurpassable. I have inherited nothing that could make a merchant of me," implying: "You are all contemptible merchants. Don't you dare pity me: I am proud of my incompetence!" As one can guess, there is another variant with reference to my artistic tastes. The trick works wonders: my very weakness is transformed into a virtue.

These games of vanity all seem to suggest that my incapacity is largely due to my imaginary self-aggrandizement. As long as this state endures, I will never have the calm and perseverance to acquire the knowledge needed to practice a profession.

These traits of superiority/inferiority started to develop from my earliest childhood. Through the force of inertia I opposed the irrevocable dictates of my parents, whose demands were in no way compensated by the affection that my sensitive nature demanded. It was not that they never loved me; rather, they imposed their idea of duty on me with excessive rigidity. I was led to look for satisfaction on my own and, instead of using my real abilities and developing them by exerting myself at school, I took refuge in idle daydreams, which could only make me apathetic and lazy. I could certainly have rebelled openly. However, because of my temperament and probably also the inacessible heights on which I placed my parents in my imagination, I preferred to oppose them deviously by indulging in passive disobedience.

Their reprimands gave my laziness a taste of sin: Baby Jesus, I was informed, was not happy. What a burden for a child—to be loved neither by the good Lord nor by his own mother! The only possible escape from all these miseries was to seek satisfaction in my own imagination, outside the extremely restricting sphere of humankind; there, I comforted myself for what, unconsciously but wholeheartedly, I considered an injustice.

My laziness was apparent throughout my school years, during which my loneliness was adorned by fanciful daydreams. Starting at age eleven or twelve, I bought novels with the little pocket money that my father gave me (and when he forgot to give me any, I would not have dared remind him for anything in the world). I remember spending hours staring into bookstore windows during the three holidays a month allowed by my provincial school. I particularly like train-station bookstores, where I could linger, hypnotized, undisturbed by the saleslady's questions, thanks to the comings and goings of travelers. My attention was drawn to the colorful jackets of the novels in the great departure hall of the Orsay station, near my home, with their promises of escape into worlds of magic and wonder. I used to take along a list, drawn up from the advertisements on the last pages of books I already owned, of titles whose resonance, strangeness, or evocative power had struck me. I would examine shelf after shelf, trying to find the book I coveted in order to make sure that its appearance was not disappointing. But luck was rarely on my side, and I avoided asking for the slightest bit of information for fear that the saleslady's suggestions might further complicate my wavering choice and increase my anxiety. I was back to square one: putting my now useless list into my pocket, I would attempt to come to a decision which was becoming more and more agonizing by the minute: "This book looks interesting, but what if it disappoints me? I hope it doesn't cost more than ten francs! I'd look pretty dumb if I asked for it, only to find out that I don't have the money! Wouldn't this other book be better? And how will the saleslady look at me if it turns out to be 'unsuitable for a child my age'?"

At a time when my classmates preferred to go out and play, I would buy novels by Frondaie, Bazin, Cherbuliez, Farrère, Dekobra, Loti, Pierre Benoît, Larrouy, Vogüe, Armandy. . . . I identified with the heroes and was bewitched by the heroines of this narrative, fictional, and sentimental literature; unknown to everyone, these figures peopled daydreams far more attractive than my lessons and homework, on which I was unable to focus my attention. The result showed up in my marks: I was always among the five or six worst students in my class.

My passive revolt was no more than an impotent escape into imagination; in turn, this escape reinforced my revolt, leading me to seek comfort in further imaginary escapism. Caught in this oscillation, my initial petty opposition to my parents' prohibitions ballooned into an ever-increasing sense of guilt, which fed on the seed of successive vanities, gradually invading my entire childhood. I can feel its effects to this very day in my laziness, incompetence, failures, and a whole retinue of defects.

My incompetence as a schoolboy, a source of humiliation vis-à-vis my classmates, was caused by the wrong motivations of my vanity. It pervaded my entire life, extending to an ever-larger area as I grew into manhood and my horizons broadened. After a series of wrong turns and failures, my academic obligations have now been replaced by my present obligations at Dictio. The environment has widened and changed, but the figure that moves in this new environment is still the same, except for a few superficial changes owing to greater age and knowledge. Wherever I go and in whatever I do, I still carry along my unchanging vanity—this vanity/motivation which, not being itself an action, does not depend on the facts of external life but instead remains fixated on the anxious attempt to justify my imperfections.

It is natural that, starting from what I feel today, I should be able to retrieve by analogy all my childhood attitudes. The only significance of delving into the past is the feeling of cohesiveness which emerges from all the wrongly motivated behaviors. The comprehensiveness of this explanation in terms of my own life experience proves that I have grasped the truth fairly accurately, in the same way as in physics the exactness of knowledge is measured by a theory's explanatory scope. What can be more important that to make sure that I am not mistaken in looking for the origin of my inner bewilderment in my vanity?

In high school, unable to stand my feelings of inferiority heightened by my bad marks, I used to despise and beat up the good students, all the while seeing myself as incomparably more valorous in my storybook daydreams than all those know-it-alls.

At the present time, my painful inability has made the atmosphere at Dictio seem to me just as unbearable as the one at school. Robert is the good student, and I would gladly beat him up. I despise him as much as I admire him, since from the heights of my fictional fancies—which have evolved into vanity about my philosophical spirituality—I see Robert as a horribly matter-of-fact and unscrupulous merchant, incapable of soaring to the lofty heights to which I am carried by my extreme sensitivity.

Classes, studies, exams—for me these were nothing but a demanding and arbitrary whim on my parents' part. It is remarkable to think that, addicted as I was to imagination, my mind had never for an instant applied itself to understanding life as it is lived by ordinary mortals: work related to a particular skill, compensated by money which determines the standard of living. My parents, in spite of their wealth, their mansions and their estates, never displayed their riches in everyday details. I thought of myself as coming from a poor family compared with certain classmates who flaunted luxury in small things but whose parents' income was actually quite modest. I envied these small belongings—clothes, toys—so much and was so ashamed of my own that I sometimes refused to appear in public. However, it never occurred to me that by passing my exams I could gain access to a career which would enable me to achieve a good position and earn the money needed to buy all the beautiful things I coveted. As for our mansions, servants, or daily bread—my family's style of living and assets were, to my child's eyes, as natural, normal, and immutable as the fact of having a nose, mouth, and ears. In the same way, tradition dictated that my parents should want me to graduate from one of the best schools.

Now, thirty years later, I am absolutely dumbfounded at this somewhat hypnotic state of obliviousness in which I spent my childhood! I would not believe it had I not experienced it personally and had psychology not pointed out its origins to me: blind vanity which no longer even notices inherited privileges, however spectacular these may be, seduced as it is by the attraction of all that has been denied to it, however mediocre. Inadequacies attempt to find imaginary overcompensation. To the apathetic personality, the most enviable quality is disinhibition, even in its tritest form. Yet this overvaluation does not trigger the acquisitive reflex—not only is freedom in relationships with others seen as a gift forever withheld but, because of the need for imaginary compensation, it is also discredited as a sign of mediocrity in all its forms, no matter how legitimate. This pseudo-superiority, unrelated to any real merit, was so much a part of me as to make any reference to my inadequacy seem a crime of high treason and any reaction impossible, in the same way that the unquestionable leaves no room for calling into question.

Shielded by my family and its privileged status, my vanity was never exposed to attacks from the outside world, at least not in the form of the struggle for existence. Thus I could prolong my childhood apathy with impunity and allow my imagination to drift along. This situation persisted for a considerable length of time. How I ever managed to graduate from high school I do not know, but afterward I was pushed by tradition into a military career, the least suited to my abilities and inclinations. Attracted mostly by the prestige of wearing a uniform, I was totally unaware of its actual demands. As in high school, I was once again part of a sheltered group of people who did not have to worry about making a living. Only the fight for survival could perhaps have woken me from my stupor.

Ten years later, upon leaving the army, life towered before me, driving home the contrast between fantasy and reality. Throughout my entire childhood my vanity, shielded from social reality, had sprawled out in a state of false bliss. Finally exposed to the world and its demands, it was cornered into having to defend its positions at every step. My parents were dead, and I was responsible for my own material security. Difficulties loomed up all around me and refused to yield to the superiority I felt. Ever on the lookout for its meager triumphs, my ruffled vanity could now spread out over a considerably larger area, as its flow of accusatory superiority and ebb of sentimental inferiority involved me in ever more anxious conflicts.

In the midst of all this vain agitation devoid of any real aim or hope, I had to find a haven in which to let my fantasies unfold relatively unchallenged. I cultivated a knack for painting in an attempt to become an artist, hoping to dodge the test of the business world where only by asserting one's practical skills can one avoid defeat and where efficiency is measured in terms of money earned. Since great artists, however, often know only failure, I could claim to be their equal irrespective of any success. The absurdity of this idea led me to play the part of the nonconformist eccentric, for which I ended up paying a high price soon enough.

Even though I never flaunted a "Saint-Germain-des-Prés"[4] extravagance in my tastes, I took advantage of my newly acquired self-importance to rebel against my family's traditions. I am pretty certain that a genuine feeling for truth in me was shocked at the conventional contradictions in my environment's judgments. I finally rebelled openly. This belated rebellion was all the more extreme because it had been restrained during my childhood by glorified submission.

An eloquent example is my scandalous marriage, which took place at this time.

How indecisive I must have been deep inside when I told my mother of my plans to marry a woman I had met in artistic circles, who on top of being of more than humble origins was also a foreigner and somewhat of an adventuress to boot. My mother's tactless reaction—her threat of depriving me of family prerogatives which I was entitled to and bestowing them on my younger brother—caused me to

[4]An area in Paris where upper-class bohemian intellectuals hang out in cafés. (Translator's note)

make up my mind immediately and fly in the face of convention. I was banished from my family and from my social circle.

The backlash was quite violent: after the miserable experience of living with my wife was over—my wife who, in the final analysis, had not been freely chosen but imposed to me by circumstances, my hedonism and the attraction of her surprising whimsicality—I found myself alone, deprived of my family's support. My art, my wife, my family ties—everything was slipping away. I was distraught; I had been wounded in the very depths of my self-esteem. My fall was all the more abrupt since I had attempted to stand out through my rebellion. All my reverse conformism rose up to scoff at me!

What was my reaction? Far from becoming aware of the vanity of my behavior and delving into my motives—I was quite incapable of doing this at the time—all that occurred to me was to do an about-face and go back to my family, to submit to its demands and look for a "serious" job. This is the reason I accepted Robert's proposals.

Thus, my entry into Dictio corresponds only to a new manifestation of my anxiety, an anxiety which continues to hem me in all the more. Ever since my childhood, my wild imagination has led me away from the realities of being human. For me, they constitute a foreign world, an unknown and hostile structure. Suffering from my lack of insight and frozen into my ineptness, I would naturally feel pushed away by real life. How could I let my life go by and negate every form of active existence without being haunted by the frightening specter of death? It is a basic need to aspire to actively seize life in one of its concrete forms; but whenever I tried to come out of my inactivity, anxiety would drive me to chaotic agitation and terror would completely prevent me from persevering. Unable as I was to find a sane form of activity, I rushed headlong into business to prove to myself that I was capable of living in the hope of bringing about the admiration I yearned for—all the while knowing that I would never get it in this way. This is the deepest motive for my now playing the businessman so awkwardly. But no matter what path I might have been tempted to enter, as long as my motives remained the same I would scarcely have considered it worthy of myself to simply prove my efficiency but would instead have felt compelled to equal and even supplant those more capable and experienced than I. This has inevitably led me to failures, the terrifying proof of my inability to do what I most long for, to be a part of life.

Since I perceive my friend Robert both as the embodiment of the abilities I envy and as a living reproof of my own inability, his everyday presence by my side necessarily transforms him into a phantom of my own creation, firmly rooted in my mind, relentlessly condemning me by constant comparison. How could I avoid wanting to turn the situation around and, not really being able to, trying to reach my goal through imaginary justification?

Seeking to escape from elations which only bring humiliations in their wake, my vanity set out to find another realm of comparison where it could get its own back—a realm in which incompetence manifested less dramatically than on the material plane, in which it could savor its triumphs. None was more appropriate than the realm of mind to which psychology had given me access. Taking refuge in it, I could get even with Robert and accuse him as much as I wanted. Robert had become for me a despicable being who had agreed to sell his soul for money.

Faced with failure, I once again sidestepped the real issue: the artist turned businessman returned presumptuously to the realm of mind.

This new about-turn is no doubt due to the temptation to use my interest in psychology to condemn not only Robert but everyone who has been successful in business. Does this mean that psychology is no more than a pretext I turn to my vanity's advantage? Yet it would be no more rel-evant to study the theory of motives than to study any other ideology, were it not that theoretical understanding leads directly to a practical technique I can apply every day to ob-serve the way my vanity flares up and become familiar with its countless masks and disguises. Theoretical knowledge is ineffective without the effort to apply it; its application alone is conclusive. A theory is true because good sense—as opposed to common sense—has always known it without knowing the theory. Good sense is defined as the ability to avoid getting all keyed up. To live without either nervous or ordinary overexcitement, whether or not one needs a the-ory, is to connect with the meaning of truth, whereas to know the theory and to pride oneself on this is to go against the meaning of life. I would thus be well advised to identify the undeniable part of vanity in my present interest for the-ory in order to better comprehend the real practical benefit I hope to derive from it.

Perversely, I turn my knowledge of psychology against Robert and accuse him of not being my equal, whereas I should in fact use the sense of balance and calm it provides exclusively in view of achieving the competence and au-thority I envy in him. I not only turn the knowledge I have acquired against Robert, but generally feel entitled to think of myself as an insightful and wise person for whom the depths of the mind no longer hold any secrets, in contrast to my surroundings, which I falsely see as a place of blind pas-sions and trivialities. This absurd need for one-upmanship is the very same reason which once led me to study astrology and theosophy.

I end up placing myself in the ludicrous position of the antipsychological psychologist. No matter how implausi-ble the blind man turned hunter may seem, he is neverthe-less impressive with his outfit, his gaiters and his gun. While parading as a psychologist, I still cling to this com-petitive game of imaginary comparison which has cost me so dearly. My accusation of others conceals a snarl of jealousy. My effort is divided—it fluctuates between the anguish of feeling inferior and the impatience of reaching for supremacy; my pretense of wisdom is no more than a whine of spite and impotence. However, the flicker of hope I felt from my very first contact with the analyst suggests that, haunted as I was by suicidal feelings and the sense of being a total, hopeless failure, my interest was so intense that my vanity consented to sacrifice itself, giving way to a longing to know the truth about the origin of my mistake. At the present time, the knowledge I have acquired takes the form of a tremendously complex tangle of true and false motivations. This intricacy is maintained by the perverse desire to fulfill, by means of the cure, the old aspirations of my vanity. My present interest in a theory in which I personally can see no flaw goes hand in hand with careful experimentation, which helps me detect my habitual patterns and begin to appreciate the facts of my daily life in a well-balanced way. The conflicts between valid and deceptive intentions is still there. Quite often still, taking advantage of my weakness, my old intentions born of my vanity gain the upper hand and try to make psychology subservient to their profit. But the relapses caused by my mistakes and the suffering which immediately follows in their wake bring me back to a more objective review of the motives of my actions, especially those which underlie my interest in the theory on which the cure is based. My daily mistakes in behavior are necessarily connected with the partially false vision that I have of psychology. However, if the theory is really true, re-examining my habitual patterns should provide me with relief.

My genuine interest in overcoming my failings and achieving composure pushes me to experiment further. Only through experimentation can I see for myself whether psychology is right or wrong.

I do not claim to be able to overcome my excitability already, but I am beginning to cope with it. I have learned quite effectively to stop the imaginary sequences related to my active shortcomings, a form of impotent rage which I used to dwell on endlessly in the past. Sometimes I am even able to get over an insult to my pride immediately. Yesterday, for instance, Robert started to talk politics in a peremptory tone. Not only was he getting on my nerves for coming across as a supreme judge, but I also felt personally provoked because he was going over a topic we had debated several times before, knowing full well how different our two points of view are. My first thought was to oppose him, but I held back; aware of my aggressive mood, I suddenly realized what a foolish situation I was about to get sucked into. My aggravation at being contradicted, triggered off by Robert's somewhat provocative self-assurance, had put me in a state of turmoil and would have made me systematically contradict Robert by advancing opinions I am unsure of or even disagree with. It would have been easy for Robert to refute my quibbles with quibbles of his own, putting me as usual in an unbearable position, quite the opposite of the triumph I would have expected. At that point, detecting the irritation in my voice, he would have taken advantage of my weakness to further emphasize his superiority. I would not have been able to help fuming with resentment, while not daring to reprove him openly for acting the way I myself would really have liked to act.

Throughout our conversation, these thoughts and many other similar ones replaced the habitual ruminations of my anxiety and gave way to a sort of humor which enabled me to listen patiently, even with some interest, to my friend's boasting. Nonetheless, I was quite far from being genuinely tolerant; my attitude let show far too much condescension, the petty vengeance of my mistreated vanity.

Now that I can stand back and think about it, what I have just discovered about my own and Robert's motives and about my way of correcting them seems so simple and obvious in its effectiveness that I am amazed that I had never seen it before. My difference with respect to other people might actually lie in their good sense, which enables them to experience these obvious facts subconsciously, without needing to articulate them. Yet Robert, who is surely not a high-strung person—at least not as intensely or in the same way as I—seems to be no freer than I from his undeniable need to triumph; he is perhaps only more skilled at satisfying it. But he satisfies it at my expense, because I am weak enough to lend myself to it. When he is faced with someone stronger than he, I have often seen him take on the same annoyed, sheepish look I know so well, without at any point becoming aware of his unquestionable mistake. His arrogance does not always protect him. Is it then the very flagrancy of our mistakes that conceals them from our awareness? Their unceasing repetition deludes us into seeing them as perfectly natural and effective attitudes of defense and attack—as long as we are unable to foresee their disastrous consequences. Why do I need to rack my brains to know who Robert is and carry on about his far too obvious delusion? The real point is to understand who *I* am and to see the deluded pride that has blinded me all my life—and still blinds me all too often—to the obvious distress that results from my mistakes. This might be the only way to understand others, since each of us suffers from this distress, which forms—or rather deforms—our common existence. It may be both the most obvious and the most hidden point, the one most hidden from our pride because it is so painfully obvious.

The fact remains that by monitoring and putting order into my motives I have been able for once to foresee and avoid one of the countless, apparently unimportant mistakes which I was about to make once again. This method, by throwing light on my internal upheavals and their repercussions in myself and in my environment, gives rise to an important and essentially living study—a practice of life, on the level of both feelings and reactions. In the final analysis, it is this aspect of the study that makes it attractive to me in spite of its theoretical aspect. It also makes it painful— although tremendously reassuring since it removes any hint of unsurmountable fatality from my feelings of inadequacy or dissatisfaction. Theory only helps round things out; it captures one's intellectual interest and answers the need to understand life's problems in a coherent fashion. However, it is useful only if precise insight into my daily habitual patterns is magnified by the global vision of a sane orientation. When all is said and done, the important thing is to achieve tranquillity, to make friends with myself, to learn to bear life, and—taking the previous example as one problem among many—to be able to listen to Robert or anyone else quibble away without being caught up in childish rage.

« 3 »

Geneviève

At the cocktail party where we met, Geneviève and I chatted for quite a while. Sometime later I bumped into the friend who had introduced us and asked him about this young woman. "You've really made a good impression on her, old boy! Each time I see her she talks about you."

He explained that she was an expatriate who had sought refuge in France. She was divorced and lived quite modestly with her twelve-year-old daughter on the miraculously saved remnants of her great fortune. She was, he said, a very gentle and kind-hearted woman.

I pricked up my ears on being told of the good impression I had made on her and managed to get her phone number without making it too obvious that my imagination was already running after her. Actually, only my pride had been flattered, for I really would not have been able to recognize this woman, who had become no more than a vague memory of blond hair, youthful figure, and pleasant conversation.

I called her up and arranged a date. On the appointed evening—about six months ago—I took her out to dinner and then went dancing. We kissed and she came over to my place.

Geneviève is a sweet person, considerate, intelligent, and serious. For her the war had been especially tragic. She had lost everything: her country, her parents, her wealth.

She smiles at the importance we French attach to material goods: "They are gone so quickly!" She harbors no bitterness and does not seem to suffer excessively from her difficult situation.

What rare qualities! She would no doubt make a very congenial mistress, with whom one could easily picture a life of sincerity, inner comfort, and mutual trust, the type of intimacy which allows genuine feelings to blossom.

This is far from being the case. With her, I feel tense and shut off from any form of spontaneity. Haunted as I am by the fear that she wants to take over my life, my first reaction is often to withhold any proof of affection lest she interpret it as a commitment. My reserve is constantly reinforced by her frequent references to her loneliness and her need to have people around her and feel loved—when she is not telling me more directly that my detachment makes her think that I am only with her to satisfy my sexual desire. At heart, I am afraid of not being able to withstand her emotional demands, especially since I tend to see them as strategies to monopolize me—a trap I have fallen into before. But just as I dread giving in to Geneviève's emotionalism, I am also afraid of losing her if I refuse to play her game.

My desire to avoid repeating the overly sentimental adventures of my past should perhaps have led me to seek out loose women, but a life of promiscuity would have flown in the face of the moral principles which have always hemmed me in. Refusing to show Geneviève the tenderness she seems to deserve makes me feel not only guilty but also crude and afraid of being judged as such.

Unable to rid myself of my mental reservations, I am constantly on my guard, in a state of tension hardly conducive to enjoyment.

"Good-looking" men, I feel, are expected to have amorous conquests and to perform. In the past, egged on by this vanity, I would often think that the woman I was with was only waiting for me to take her by storm with my maleness, and I would feel obliged to play the conqueror. An inner voice, however, would not stop whispering and opposing me. "Will you be able to pull this off?" it would murmur, anxiously considering the task imposed by my vanity. "And what if this woman does not want anything from you and rejects you? Won't you look dumb?" Often enough, I have laughed at these fears on seeing the feeble resistance put up by the woman who had, after all, melted in my arms—but at other times I really would meet with rejection. To hide my embarrassment, I would sometimes become brutal and in-sulting, especially since I was only pretending to be cynical. I remember one evening when, in order to avoid losing face, I terrorized the girl I was with and threatened to rough her up. However, my fear of losing the respect I crave would generally lead me to play the opposite role and apologize profusely for my ever so forgivable impetuousness: "You're so beautiful!" I would say. I would almost congratulate her for having rejected me, since this made her all the more ex-ceptional and enticing. The way was now clear for me to make much of my uncommon thoughtfulness and lofty principles through moralistic preaching.

When I recall my teenage days, my long-term rela-tionships seem on the whole to have been affectionate affairs. In spite of my timid desire to keep up with my class-mates, I never really had a high regard for their offhanded-ness, which seemed trivial to me: "How is ti possible to treat women with such contempt!" Seeing sex as something beastly unless it was ennobled by feelings, I found physical enjoyment impossible without a veneer of overidealization —which actually applied more to my exquisite deference than to my girlfriend's qualities. It is staggering to see what vanity can do to a man: my search for admiration gave rise to waves of sentimentality.

When I was younger, my mistresses' social status usu-ally meant that I could give unbridled rein to my penchant for sentimentality without getting too committed since they were either married or else known for the free lives they led. As an officer, my impending departure for the colonies underscored the temporary aspect of the relationship. But the split between the lofty feelings I would give vent to without ever committing myself or taking responsibility and the secret reservations which really determined the type of love affairs I chose made these situations very painful, since I actually had an extreme craving for perfection.

Why did I never settle on a girl from my own background? I could have married her and avoided the obsessive fear of getting a woman pregnant that accompanies illicit sex. But this is to misunderstand the image I had of girls. As embodiments of Purity they were so untouchable that even to brush against one would have been a promise of marriage. But the idea of marriage immediately brought up the disgust I felt at committing myself, for, in spite of my apparent sentimentality, at heart I felt that no woman was worthy of me, exceptional being that I am. What would people say when I told them I was engaged to a girl who was short of being the prettiest, wealthiest, or noblest of all—in short, one who was not the best match!

The utter fancifulness of my superiority turned my yearning for marriage into an obsessive and unattainable fancy. I so desperately wish to get married that whenever a woman is mentioned to me and her beauty extolled, she inevitably starts to haunt my daydreams. My imagination instantly transforms her into the ideal mate, the woman I will be bound to forever by a love that can only grow with time and fill my entire life with rapture! But unfortunately, as soon as I actually meet her I discover a blemish which makes her unacceptable to my eyes. No woman ever finds favor with me; all are proscribed by my vanity. My desire to get married grows more impatient the older I get (I am now forty). Young women, who represent my ideal more than mature women, are ever harder to come by, and I am tormented by the anxiety and the guilt of not being able to create the home that every human being instinctively longs for and that most people know how to create, some better than others.

My propensity for oversentimentality, far from being a sign of real depth of feeling, is only a form of perversity. The first step toward freeing oneself from these motivations is to see their absurdity with humor. Even though I dread this sentimentality, whose dangers I am starting to become familiar with, I am still too attracted to it not to be its prisoner.

This is how I understand my resistence to Geneviève's captivating sentimentality which I am afraid of being dragged into. I would like to avoid the trap, but my old reflexes and behavior patterns are still there, and my anxious tension freezes me into an unbearably self-conscious stance of rigid distrust.

Although my imaginary distrust of Geneviève makes me feel like running away from her, I do not do so for fear of losing a devoted mistress whom it would be difficult to replace. The pleasure I feel in her arms is inhibited by the agonizing struggle between sensual excitement and guilt. As tortured as our relations may be, they at least satisfy my physical need and spare me the trouble and disappointments of looking for pickups.

My imagination, always easily unleashed and quick to boil over, has pushed me into pitiful adventures countless times, dragging me onto the streets in search of a chance encounter or, in desperation, a prostitute. But on the actual scene of my imagined exploits everything falls apart and I cannot help seeing my moral decay. My inhibitions take over completely—I watch myself grow awkward and tongue-tied and the woman I want seems suddenly inaccessible. I am filled with shame at the idea of holding a prostitute in my arms. Faced with a sordid reality, my plunge into inhibition is all the greater because my daydreams had vanquished all obstacles. There is nothing left for me but the righteous comfort of telling myself that my very failure bears witness to my exceptional integrity. Even though this idea should make me want to give up the pursuit of such adventures, the very act of renunciation floods my mind anew with fanciful seduction scenes.

The memory of such adventures, together with the anxiety of once again having to deal with disappointing situations, makes me afraid of breaking up with Geneviève in spite of the dissatisfaction I feel with her. In the same way that my inhibiting guilt was the cause for my past failures, my exaggerated self-importance now fills me with distrust for Geneviève. These constant upheavals make me wander about aimlessly in a completely illusory and phantasmagorical world, torn between two personalities. Just like Stevenson's hero, I am either Jekyll or Hyde, but never myself. One of these two contradictory characters who live within me aspires to exalted deeds, to perfect chastity, only to be replaced instantly by the other, whose sole aim is to unleash his passions. Pushed either by the saint or by the demon, I am filled with anxiety about the world and about myself since each of these characters, magnified to the point of absurdity, is neutralized by his inseparable companion's paralyzing hostility. Only by lowering considerably the unattainable expectations of my vanity can I expect to free myself from my inhibiting contradictions instead of being their victim—as I have always been in the wretched adventures I have known, mere attempts at throwing off my inhibitions, and as I still am due to my exaggerated guilt. I will only achieve unity when I am no longer tempted by contradictory desires and when all my intentions, reoriented in a saner direction, work together effectively.

In the past, I have been the helpless prey of these phenomena. The inhibiting split has extended into all areas of my life, and I have experienced it without ever understanding its scope or meaning. Attempting to rebel against my idealization of young girls, which dates back to my teenage days, I have held in my arms young virgins ready to give themselves to the seducer, without being able to take them. My guilt feelings had yet again pushed my mind away from this desirable flesh and prevented me from enjoying it— repelled not by women, but by myself. Only when a woman managed to distract me from my guilt feelings did she find in me a satisfying lover. But my ruffled vanity remembers only the setbacks.

Seeking to make up for these setbacks, my vanity led me into further disappointments. No woman could ever satisfy me, since there was always a more beautiful one, or one with a different sort of beauty. To want to possess them all meant to not really possess any. Even if I managed to allay suspicion, my unsatisfied virility would still suffer, since sexual power seems to be the supreme quality for the man who is cynically free of any inhibition. This agonizing comparison with a fantasy of cynical disinhibition heightened my inhibitedness. It is this feeling of inferiority and of shame that I feel to be the most painful; it has haunted me ever since my early teens thanks to the conventions of boastfulness which are so morbidly associated with sex. My excessively moralizing mind with its inordinate requirements of purity has given rise to guilt feelings, the essential cause of my intimidation; these are strengthened by the memories of previous experiences which contributed to build up my inhibiting anxiety. The fear of failure becomes the cause for a new form of inhibition which further prevents me from experiencing any real satisfaction.

What drives me to look for adventures is not a real need or a personal attraction for a particular woman but my deeply anguished and inhibited desire, which longs only to experience the anxious lust of my vanity's pseudo-sexuality—overstimulated or nervously inhibited. The nervous individual is trying to prove his erotic potential to himself in spite of his underlying anxiety. Pleasure is replaced exclusively by performance anxiety, the feeling of being put to the test. Fear, coupled with a choice devoid of any real feeling, can only give paltry results, leading in turn to even greater anxiety. This disastrous situation is further reinforced by the fact that, since sexual appeasement is seen as a sort of test and one's partner is reduced to being the object of an experiment, the relationship loses any incentive. Pleasure is reduced to the unsatisfying triviality of a sexual automatism seeking to escape from the spell of inhibition through artificial stimulation. Amazingly, the inhibition which was originally based on imaginary guilt has now produced paradoxical situations in which the sense of guilt and shame are really justified.

The sexual act, distorted by vanity, is personified into the ideal of virility. Severed from any motivating connections, it finds itself elevated to the status of life's central issue. However, I am more and more convinced that every act—including the sexual act—is only healthy or unhealthy as a result of the sane or insane motivations which underlie it and through which it links up with all the other issues of life.

Although it is pleasure that binds me to Geneviève, I am afraid that satisfying that pleasure will drag me into sentimental subjection, and this prevents me in fact from developing bonds of real feeling with her.

This bond between two people who are materially independent and free to determine their own lives without harming anyone and who have the same level of education, seems nonetheless forbidden to me by the fact that the sexual act, performed in fear of commitment, is in fact impure. The vanity of thinking I am exceptional prevents me from appreciating the real advantages of my relationship: physical attraction, a ground of mutual respect, the honesty of not deceiving anyone. But I need more: I need love! I would like to be loved without having to give of myself at all.

The impurity of my actions and my lack of sincerity have created a strained atmosphere between us, which has ended up arousing Geneviève's own sense of guilt. How could she help blaming herself for giving herself to me without being loved? Her pride rebels. It is no doubt the shame which she feels at allowing herself to be content merely with my carnal caresses that triggers off her irritating tendency to involve me in extreme emotionalism. To a great degree I am responsible for this. Since my wounded vanity rejects all responsibility, my nervous tendency is to lay most of the blame on her in order to vindicate myself and avoid having to admit that I am just not "up to it."

Afraid of my need for sentimentality, I become unjustly harsh and bring out Geneviève's own need for sentimentality—precisely what I am afraid of. This really makes Geneviève unsatisfactory, but the inadequacy I blame her for is actually created by my own inability to cope with the situation.

Should I break up with her? This would no doubt be a form of escape, for which I would sooner or later feel regret and shame. Besides, I would only be able to do it by being either brutal in order to hide my weakness, or else basely sentimental, self-righteously highlighting my exceptional moral qualities. The very thought of breaking up, tied in as it is with the vision of a dismal fatalism, makes me feel so abandoned that I know I would start missing Geneviève from the moment I left her. My anxiety at not being able to establish ties with a woman would only increase. To replace her I would build project upon project. I would even consider winning her back with the very emotionalism I had so far denied her. But would I not then become her toy? At that point, I would find myself in the very situation I had wanted to avoid all along.

Given my present state of mind, no solution can prove satisfactory. I must try to overcome this situation by facing it, by seeing what is actually happening inside me and trying hard to overcome the fantasies which make me entirely responsible for the dissatisfaction that I sow and reap. My nervous sentimentality is mere self-indulgence born of vanity. Perhaps everything would be all right if I could arouse in myself true feelings toward Geneviève rather than making her into an outlet for and a phantom of my inflated desires and inhibiting anxieties.

« 4 »

My Difficulties at Work

*E*ach time Robert asks me to show a possible customer one of the appliances we manufacture I have to fight a deep feeling of anguish and force myself to do it. I muddle through my demonstration, ill at ease with the customer. I feel like an aristocrat who has come down in the world, yet I am the first to affirm that no work is demeaning. In actual fact, this opinion is a mere slogan I have adopted superficially in order to show off my generosity. I submit to Robert's judgment and accept the role that he suggests for me since to refuse would be to admit my inaptitude for business. And if I were to admit the panic I feel when faced with the customer, Robert would accuse me of not being brave or energetic enough, since he himself is able to deal with the customer and command respect. So, as I set out to do my demonstration, I am gnawed by anxiety at the opinion of the imaginary accuser that Robert has become in my mind. His illusory presence follows me even in my sales tactics.

Will I manage to prove this time that I am no less competent than he? A vague hope disguises the secret certainty that I will once again be forced to tell him that the customer was not interested. I dread having to misrepresent the customer's refusal one more time, justifying myself like a schoolboy to hide my humiliating awkwardness.

However, for all my resignation at having to go

through such trials with my customers and for all the obsessive constraint that forces me to justify my failure before my partner, I feel a silent resentment at my friend, since it is on account of his demands that I was snubbed. "Who does he think he is?" My cornered vanity retreats to its most usual refuge: my ancestry. The greater the contrast with my demerit, the more I use my noble extraction as a pedestal because of its indisputable superiority over the peerage which Robert brags about. Ironically, the more I seek to triumph in this fashion, the more humiliated I feel at having to take orders from "a nobody, a wretched little country squire."

Driven along by this insoluble conflict between superiority and inferiority, my resentment grows and extends into all the situations of my life. On my way to the despised customer my arrogance prevails over my wretchedness and I fantasize about the splendid role that my social status would have secured for me in bygone days. Inevitably, my rekindled vanity leads me to condemn this age of merchants, but this self-righteous accusation turns into sentimental self-pity: "The things one has to do in this dreary day and age!"

In my pitiful attempts at superiority, I end up condemning merchants while endeavoring to become one myself!

Even though a man in my state of mind cannot possibly confront, demonstrate, convince, or sell, consciously I do my best. I make an effort to change my strategy, my gestures, my voice, to adapt my sales pitch—all in vain! The external motions I go through are mere posturing, constantly disrupted by my internal turmoil. I identify not with the role of a salesman, but with a dual personality who is both superior and inferior. Since to behave presumptuously would be out of character, I try to act like a cool and casual socialite, hiding my hesitation and fear. The customer subconsciously perceives this complicated attitude, which inevitably leads to deplorable results. I am inhibited enough by what other people might say in a social gathering; it is easy then to imagine my apprehensiveness when, opening the door to an office, I am faced with the gaze of the manager, whom I must attempt to convince. To make him appreciate all the qualities of my wares, I either ramble on about high-flying considerations which have nothing to do with the subject at hand, as if I were having a very genteel conversation; or else I dwell at length on the appliance's merits, clumsily exaggerating them. Absent-mindedly parroting a lesson learned by rote, I am thrown into a panic the moment the customer makes an objection. My systematic exaggeration, with the guilt in my voice belying the meaning of my words, conveys my lack of conviction to my customer. In addition, as soon as I find myself face to face with the customer, I start to doubt the quality of my wares. Similarly, when I was an artist, I used to find my paintings abominable the moment I showed them, even though they had seemed to me like masterpieces up to that point!

As I salesman, however, I do not benefit from the favorable prejudice enjoyed by artists, however mediocre. Sometimes, the violence of my anxiety has left me speechless, with my wandering mind preventing me from uttering a single word.

But when I really get flustered is when it comes to talking about the price! At this climactic instant the price suddenly seems exorbitant and I would gladly give my merchandise away for free. However, since the Robert in my mind does not stop watching me, I have to forge ahead anyway. I hesitate, splutter out—or trumpet out—the price, and then immediately start offering the customer all kinds of discounts in a roundabout way, stammering and mumbling in embarrassment. As my voice regains its strength, I attempt to explain to him that, not being an ordinary salesman or employee but one of the board members of the company, I can subtract the commission that is normally allowed for sales representatives. Unable to close the sale, to wrap it up, I almost always tell the customer that he must have realized, from my lack of know-how, that I am not a professional salesman. What an abomination, what a grotesque situation! Now, far from the obligation to perform, I can see it with the humor it deserves.

Back on the street, free at last, I am suddenly furious at myself. I tell myself over and over what I could and should have done. In a vain attempt to escape from these unbearably painful feelings, I take refuge once again in my haughty disdain of merchants and the times and wallow in self-pity. My thoughts inevitably turn to Robert as I try to picture a technique, copied from his, that would give me the power of conviction. Robert entrenches himself in my mind, preaching to the incompetent who has once again failed. As the image of the self-possessed character which my vanity would like me to be, this Robert makes the terrorized character which my vanity has engendered feel mortified.

In actual fact, I cannot possibly be this Robert who is symbolically perfect in business, this bloated image that only exasperates my inability. These two contradictory characters are both imaginary. Overvaluing my real titles and my imaginary qualities makes me act like a shameful and tongue-tied salesman. Since my feelings are aggravated by my imagination and my shame makes me feel utterly dejected, I aspire to become like the perfect Robert who lives in my mind and who bears only a faint resemblance to the actual person, my friend Robert. The Robert I carry within me is an obsessional fantasy that reflects my internal split. The proof that this friend/enemy is a mere phantom is that he represents both my upset vanity (whenever I would like to equal his competence) and my triumphant vanity (whenever I attribute his success to his coarseness or lack of scruples).

A supposition comes to mind—could vanity's two faces, alternatively vexed and triumphant, be the unsuspected cause of all inner states of split, including delusions and hallucinations? All I have to do is substitute Jesus or Napoleon for Robert to be considered mad. Fortunately, my critical mind is sufficiently intact so that I need have no fear of being driven by my vanity to the final, absurd climax.

I have once again confirmed how ludicrous—and also tragical—any given situation becomes when it is experienced through the filter of nervousness.

If I could detach myself from this imaginary dual personality and pull out the root of this evil, my vanity, I would become a totally different person from the phantom of perfection which I always aspire to be. Deprived of his role as a symbol, Robert would appear to me as he really is, with his good and bad sides. Since I myself would be more objective with regard to my own real shortcomings and my potential qualities, I would be able to see other people more lucidly, without being clouded over by my competitive fears and conceited aspirations. Instead of referring back to others' supposed good qualities, I would look at the unfinished person that I actually am. By endeavoring to understand my defects I would develop my good points; by making my behavior dependent on being aware of my resources I would actualize my abilities.

It was the insane hope of fulfilling my excessive aspirations which originally led me to my therapy. To the extent that I can grasp the real intentions of the treatment, I feel the obsession of my conceited aspirations vanish, to be replaced, hopefully, by more attainable goals. May the analysis succeed in delivering me from my passionate need for unlimited prestige and help me give birth to the only sane aspiration and source of real satisfaction—the desire for inner harmony.

« 5 »

Reflections

I want everything, and reality ends up denying me everything. My nervous reflexes make me hypersensitive to any stimulation from my environment which enters my mind. I am like an unreliable membrane whose vibrations are not an exact replica of the sound waves that it receives, its excessive sensitivity making it resonate off the beat and distort sounds by either muffling or amplifying them into nodes and antinodes. Sane sensitivity, on the other hand, is a process of deliberation whereby one can reach a happy medium between perceptive stimulation and active response.

Analyzing my inner motives has given me insight into the secrets of my disorderly affectivity—until now the sole determining factor in the sorry and confused existence which was the only one I knew, the only one fitted to my rudimentary perceptions. Psychological explanation may perhaps be able to create a third personality within me, capable of watching the sterile quarrels which pit two opposing personalities against each other—one inadequate and dissatisfied and the other smug and overrated, an imaginary surrogate of the satisfaction I am denied. Psychology may perhaps make me aware of my wrong motives for acting, my insane projects and their disastrous consequences; it may help me dissolve the painful split, leading at last to the emergence of a unified self manifesting through harmonious activity. This unified personality would be the genuine self, my real potential for understanding and self-actualization. "Understanding" in this case refers not to the bookish knowledge learned by rote, which my intellect, distorted by my imagination, takes delight in toying with, but to a deep sense of truth which must be reclaimed continually through the inner experience of successively acquired satisfactions.

The reason for my ongoing interest in psychology is the desire to achieve this inner appeasement.

Not everyone feels the need to resort to a method as strict as this one; a great many people already possess a certain amount of good sense, whether inborn or acquired by experience, a sort of instinctive and natural knowledge that enables them to cope with the complications of life and overcome them to the best of their satisfaction. The example of such individuals is often painful for me, and I envy them. Sometimes, when I compare myself with people who are able to live without resorting to therapy, I feel sicker and more unbalanced that I actually am—a common attitude among nervous individuals. I become the victim of emotional self-pity and end up feeling sorry for myself, which is no more than a form of ruffled vanity. How can I fight this demon of vanity other than through the weapons of mind, through reflection?

Why should I feel entitled to owning this good sense?

I already have life. It is wonderful to have been granted this experience, which continually challenges me to overcome my insane attitudes. Instead of casting sidelong glances at other people's behavior and ranting against the unfairness of my lot, I should realize just how fair it actually is, since it forces me to earn this privilege instead of just taking it. All my behavior bespeaks my sense of being entitled to this privilege: my feeling of social superiority; my rebellion against the obligation to earn my living; the idea that no woman is worthy of me and that I am the most outstanding of men, even if I have done nothing and never will be able to do anything to justify this puffed-up claim, the cause of all my miseries.

This need for privileges, with its inherent risk of ineffectiveness, crops up in the position I take with respect to my treatment. I was able to observe this yesterday while talking to my friend A.T., a man full of good sense (although he criticizes psychology without knowing anything about it).

Yesterday, like so many other times in similar situations, I despaired at noticing that, my psychological preoccupations notwithstanding, other people's good sense helps them distinguish sanity from insanity in the details of daily life much more clearly than I. This comparison would certainly never come to mind if my vision of the goal and means of the analysis were more accurate; it arises whenever, for vanity's sake, I try to use my as yet quite inadequate knowledge to compel recognition from others. Taking pride in a knowledge that is still too global and theoretical to justify my scoffing at those I deem incapable of understanding, I demand that they acknowledge the depth and shrewdness of my judgments. Thus, I am actually misinterpreting and misusing my knowledge by emptying it of its objective truth. By turning psychological knowledge, which one could call the food of the mind, into food for my affectivity, I attain the opposite of the level-headed judgment I long for. Driven by the pleasure of arguing, I venture into areas I am not familiar with and have not yet experienced. To prove my point I distort the facts and thus lose the possibility of accurate reasoning. In this state of mind I am concerned not with truth, but with prestige—with being in the spotlight rather than with simply and freely presenting the results of my experience, the only way to have the person I am talking to be interested in and perhaps even agree with what I am saying. Instead of my obtaining the agreement I compulsively expect, my own inadequacy jumps up at me and sparks the obsessive feeling of being worthless. In despair I turn against psychology. Aroused, my underlying obsessive doubt explodes in accusation: "What kind of teaching is this that collapses at the slightest objection?"

Only analysis can enable me to understand the motives that lead to such states of exasperation; its explanation offers a means to overcome these painful situations. It is obvious that I seek satisfaction; my delusion lies in being content with the paltry satisfactions of my vanity, which turn into suffering and distress. Thus, I lose even the vision of simple, sane satisfactions. However, the satisfaction that surpasses and encompasses all others is the search for the truth about oneself, for this search is a trial of courage, a test of one's actual capacity to overcome the difficulties of daily living and the anxieties that go along with it. The search for true satisfaction is surely an essential task since it is no doubt valid and beneficial for every human being. By conferring the power to master the illusions of one's passions, it frees one from all forms of bondage to others' opinions and criticisms. By no longer depending on the contradictory opinions that prevail in the world, I will be able to acquire the calm competence that will help me bear others' objections and criticisms without the need to argue back and without being so put out by them that the only way out that occurs to me in my panic is the shame-faced disavowal of my experience.

Lastly, in whatever situation—my working relationship with Robert; the customer I approach, terror-stricken; the friend I argue with—my anxiety about other people's opinions, my vain desire to appear rather than to be, never fails to pursue me, making me feel crushingly inferior.

I also need to understand that the apathetic excesses of my real inferiorities are ambivalently contradicted on the level of my inner motives by my excesses of haughty superiority.

Thus, it may very well be true that these purely imaginary games, in which humiliated vanity and triumphant vanity alternatively get the upper hand, do in fact secretly determine and motivate the whole gamut of psychopathic states.

« 6 »

Inner Contradictions

I am starting to see that the point—perhaps the main point—of the analysis is to look into the motives for the anxious inhibition that grips me in every possible situation.

This inhibition has increased noticeably ever since I took charge of selling appliances. But how does it happen that, as far back as I can remember, I have from time to time felt suddenly relaxed in some situations? I had this experience again this morning in a customer's office. My conversation with the customer flowed easily; I came up with persuasive arguments and actually managed to convince him. My inhibition, rather than paralyzing me to the point of making me stammer, turned into glibness, perhaps under the influence of the warm welcome I had received. This lopsided attitude could just as easily have jeopardized the favorable outcome of my demonstration, as has happened several times before. My inner inadequacy actually persists, albeit under a triumphant guise. I was not to be spared the proof of this—my partner provided it to me. Back at the office, when I told Robert about my success, he first congratulated me, then changed the subject and, sure enough, within two or three sentences, had managed to puncture my arrogance. I dejectedly retreated once more into an obstinate, humiliated, indignant silence.

Were these couple of sentences Robert uttered really hostile and malicious? Were they really meant to belittle my pathetic success and demolish the triumphant attitude he perceived in my gestures, my motions, my verbosity? Quite possibly—quite probably even. His own vanity, while less inflated or hypersensitive than mine, might very well have squirmed at seeing me succeed and especially at seeing me make a display of my triumph—not only because this is in itself absurd and intolerable, but also for fear that one day I might take delight in that role and, abandoning my submissive stance, consider myself his equal or even be so bold as to act superior, a privilege he has so ably claimed as his right, thanks to my inadequacy. But I am no doubt off the track with my acrimonious and somewhat exaggerated suspicions. Unfortunately, the moment vanity takes over under one of its many shapes or masks, human relations lose all cordiality and we turn into challenged challengers.

But that is not the question, at least not at this point. What is at stake is how to identify the cause for my being at the mercy of two or three sentences uttered by Robert in what I suspect to be an aggressive frame of mind. I am convinced that this overdependence with regard to other people's intentions, whether benevolent or malicious, is the most secret cause of my weakness with my customers and in any situation, whether favorable or not.

The main thing would then be not so much what happens to me, but first and foremost my habit of reacting with resentment.

I feel very strongly at this point that this represents a complete reversal of my usual ideas about my morbid state. The cause of my shortcomings, my general feeling of discomfort, my illness, lies deep within myself. As long as I conceal it I am unable to grasp it—but the more I cover it up, the more it reasserts itself, unsurmountable and obsessive.

I do not mean to say that external situations are totally blameless, for they are what triggers my inhibition or overexcitement. But would this be possible if there were not a deep-seated, preexisting cause within me, if my ruminations had not created a buildup of overemphasized and inhibited resentments, always ready to explode? The only thing that can make me deny this secret mistake is my vanity, which leads me to try to prove my innocence by laying the blame first on situations, on my environment—in other words, on "others" and their behavior toward me. What can be more tempting than to justify oneself for vanity's sake—and what can be more disastrous? For the first time in my life, I feel the enormous weight of the word *vanity*. Its blinding seduction is what makes us all more or less distorted in our inmost depths and what leads us to create—by interaction—all the situations we suffer from and complain about. Perhaps the most harmful mistake is precisely to think that life amounts to a series of external situations rather than realizing that it is always pulsating within us, within me—that it runs in me and belongs to me, that it is all my various feelings and resentments, hopes and fears, joys and anxieties, my fleeting insights and my far too habitual blindness born of vanity.

But who am I to speak in general of mistakes and truth? I should be content to simply detect my own disastrous mistake the better to grasp my own particular truth, the truth about myself and my life. If the only causes of my suffering were external situations and other people's behavior, how could I ever hope to overcome it? If these causes were external to me, I could only sink deeper into my helpless anger, my morbid state. On the other hand, if I acknowledge that the seat of the trouble is within me, it follows that the remedy must also be within me. It is up to me, and to me alone, to mobilize it, no matter how painful. The thing to do is to cut through blindness born of vanity. It is much more painful to deal with the consequences of this blindness than to avoid them by acknowledging my weakness or my relative strength, without overstatement, each time I am faced with a difficult or favorable situation, each time I fail or succeed!

Nobody has only weak or only strong points. My vain guilt inhibits my strength by suggesting that I should have no flaws and no shortcomings. By demanding the impossible of me, it makes me feel utterly bewildered in the midst of my anxious feelings of inferiority and aspirations to superiority, of my humiliations and triumphs. It splits up my emotional life into contradictory resentments that wear themselves out in a secret, fruitless struggle. This is the essential mistake of my life, of which all the accidental mistakes and inadequate actions are only the unavoidable consequences. The remedy lies in becoming aware of and familiar with my mistake and its disastrous effects. This awareness has allowed me to see that one day, after having made the necessary effort, I may eventually rise up from my present state of ruin due to my imagination and walk at last on the solid ground of reality.

It is only too obvious to me that, whether in terms of success in business, my relationship with Robert, or my behavior in general, I am always flipping back and forth between one pole of the ambivalence and the other.

The law of ambivalence that rules the nervous individual has been explained to me several times during analysis; my preliminary understanding, however, is still too vague and theoretical. Nevertheless, it seems to me that for once my understanding has taken on a new shape—that is, revitalizing ideas which fill me with their clarity and which I know cannot fail to evolve into actively determining factors, motivations for healing. Prepared by the explanation, the sudden transformation of theoretical thinking into revitalizing ideas happens through successive confrontations with events in my life. My infrequent successes as a salesman are no doubt the cause for the extravagant intensity of the swing between both poles of the ambivalence—inferiority/superiority, humiliation/triumph, etc. I am still so struck by this discovery that I cannot take my mind off it; it has triggered an unceasing flow of insights.

Without the magic power of imagination, vanity would not have a leg to stand on. Since imagination is capable of going beyond all the limits of reality, hope, in an effort to fixate on something it can use as a symbol, unavoidably flares up just as excessively as despair did when it was being overemphasized. This is why the exuberant joy of momentarily shedding inhibition felt to me as if I had suddenly been touched with a magic wand. I had the intense feeling that everything was very easy after all; that approaching a customer, making a sale, throwing off inhibitions, and being successful in business and everything else were, in fact, just a trick one had to learn. The trickery and guile that I scorn in Robert had turned into a weapon I could use to triumph by undermining his arrogance with my own. This would involve only discovering the right scheme, as if being healed forever were just a matter of knowing the right pill to swallow.

The magic of words! A trick—that is all I need! Real efforts aimed at overcoming inhibition by examining my motives seem pointless. The effectiveness I long for so much seems to me now to be mine for good. I have managed to bring the superiority I granted Robert down to the level of a simple mechanical process. But actually, the notion of a trick seems to be the key to the formulas taught by a whole body of literature. "How to Make Friends," "How to Acquire Will Power," "How to Succeed in Life," etc. These books preach a cool self-confidence through posing and deportment, based on a sort of Coué-type method involving, for instance, continual self-suggestion: "I am strong . . . I am strong." But have I not also seen that self-suggestion is underpinned by the ambivalence of anxiety: "What if I'm not strong?" With such methods, successes are bound to be followed by defeats. Worse than that, these methods will even produce future defeats, since the slightest inadequacy will be charged with such a poignant sense of disappointment that illusion will give way to disillusionment,

exaggerated hopes to exaggerated despair. The temptation
to pin my hopes on a trick to be learned is just a new manifestation of my old state of disillusionment, which I had
sunk into to a degree that now seems inconceivable. Going
from soothsayers to astrologers, I had ended up floundering
in the limitless visions of theosophy. What I was looking
for was a lighthouse that would show me the way. But the
bewildered desire to find my bearings could only lead me to
its ambivalent reversal, to an ever-greater bewilderment.

Now I understand that all these delusions, as well as so
many others which enslave the nervous personality, are subject to the law of ambivalence since they are produced by the
symbol-making power of a primitive magical and animistic
layer that seems to survive in a dormant state in all of us. Its
subconsciously motivating force would be revived by the
nervous individual's never-ending daydreams and fantasies,
which plunge his mind into a dreamlike state. To find their
bearings in life, primitive people, for instance, seem to resort to magical explanations, which end up determining
and motivating all their activities. Might not these taboos,
apparently unwarranted suppositions, actually be collective
motivations aimed at preserving the exuberant primitive
mind from the dangers of ambivalence? It occurs to me that
in taboos, the two poles of obsession—hope and fear—are
not dissolved but magically conjured through religious rit-
ual in such a way that neither of them can be actively
expressed; they are at once forbidden and tolerated. Take
the anthropology of rituals, for instance. While it is true
that we are no longer a primitive people, aggressiveness still
persists in overemphasized forms, held in check by religious
magic and the often somewhat moralistic and overstated
love that religions impose. These taboos no longer hold,
however; they may have become too complicated, raised to
the status of ideologies and bolstered by sophistries and
dogma. The two poles of the ambivalence have split apart.
Exacerbated moralism is now being driven back by exacer-

bated, trivializing amorality, complete with its own arsenal of sophistries, which have become conventional wrong justifications. The meaning of life, its value, is being called into question. Values, degraded into ambivalences, now serve only to foster vain, game-ridden discussions. The feeling of helplessness due to the ambivalent contradiction of collective motivations is reflected in individuals, with society divided into two ambivalent groups: on the one hand, nervous individuals anxiously and painfully searching for an orientation which they are able to find only in delusions; on the other, trivialized individuals, hardly prone to delude themselves, searching for opportunities to satisfy their unbridled desires.

But I see that I have once again been carried away by my tendency to dwell on the scheming behavior of others rather than analyzing my own. Our actions can take many forms but our motives are all the same. I can recognize in myself the motives of trivialized individuals since it is, after all, these people whom I envy. Yes, I do secretly envy their unleashed appetites, even if I consider them unhealthy and consciously condemn their scheming. In my fantasies, I am at once moralistic and amoral, unable to dissolve the extremes of ambivalence and allow my healthy desires to blossom harmoniously. I live under the magical spell of contradictory taboos; my actions, both inhibited and overemphasized, are in fact no more than rites and ceremonies. This, beyond the shadow of a doubt, is the ultimate cause of the nervousness which sentences me to feed forever on delusions.

Deluded as I am, I occasionally manage to delude others. My tricks and superstitions, the warnings and omens I receive from situations and events, come not only from the imaginative projection of my anxieties, but also from the obsession of my desires charged with insatiable greed. If by chance I hit a series of green lights (especially at one particular intersection) on my way to the office in the morning, I sometimes interpret this as a omen that I will have a lucky day and be successful in all my undertakings. The same thing happens when I find good news in the morning mail. These auspicious circumstances intoxicate me with an euphoria that gives me the power to overcome all obstacles. But the obstacles I have thus overcome in my imagination do not disappear. The euphoria of my pseudo-disinhibition is merely an omen of future disappointment and dejection.

During these moments of euphoric disinhibition, I welcome the slightest favorable prompting from my environment with tremendous gratitude. My shyness disappears along with my arrogant attitude. I am flooded with waves of sentimentality and brotherly love. I feel a sense of warmth, finally free from life's icy exclusion. Life is no longer hostile—now it smiles at me. My fears and terrors are over.

Even if they know the way I am, other people still get a mistaken impression on seeing my euphorical disinhibition. This would obviously not be possible if I was unremittingly paralyzed and mute with terror. I am often amazed to find out that other people have a better opinion of my abilities than I myself. Actually, their fundamental warmth and indulgence toward me set my mind at ease and give me the feeling of putting up a relatively good show. They are only judging the facade of my appearances—what do they know of my secret anguish? At best, they probably take me for an eccentric misfit. Misfit with respect to what? To my caste, to the rules of the game of the society I live in, to the conventions that prevail all over the world? Yes, I do long to fit in as best as possible, because it is painful to live one's life as an outcast—excluded, isolated, barely tolerated. It is true that I both rebel against and give into excess, that I am always ready to make all sorts of concessions, precisely in order to be tolerated. Ambivalence is everywhere, and this contradiction between belief and doubt, between revolt and submission, is perhaps the basic cause of our widespread feeling of despair. Do we not all criticize conventionalism? Do we not all take part in endless arguments in which each person wants to impose his or her point of view, often mere conventional beliefs, scraps of ideas picked up here and there? These platitudes—amalgamated as well as can be expected into opinions—are expressed in submissive or rebellious attitudes. We all passionately defend our own points of view as if we were the only ones who knew the real meaning of life. Does life really have a meaning? And if so, would we not all be misfits with regard to life's meaning? Not fitted to experience its meaning, not even fitted to look for it and find it as long as the quarrel of excessively conventional ideas lasts.

I am prone to think that these conventions and vain arguments are themselves no more than tricks and superstitions, a way of putting up a front. All around me there are people who are brilliant talkers. I envy them, dismayed at my own inferiority. I see myself as the most disadvantaged, maladjusted, incapable, and miserable of beings. But their conceit and assurance, so crushing—could they not be just a front? Could it not be that I am confusing their behavior with their inner feelings, their true nature—just as my friends, not seeing my inner confusion, get the wrong impression and judge me by my moments of euphoric disinhibition? There are obviously genuine inferiorities and superiorities, on which the scale of talents and qualities is based. But in my case, my excessive inferiority is linked to an excessive desire for superiority. Might not others' ostentatious display of their superiorities be a mask for their own underlying inferiorities? To varying degrees, inner confusion seems to be our common lot as long as our love of argument remains intact, whether we prefer to talk to ourselves or to others, whether we are shy or brilliant. Might not the vanity and conventional sterility of all our discussions be the outcome of our inner conflicts, which we should face clearly before voicing our ideas about life and its meaning or lack of meaning?

I have just reread my notes. While condemning people who love to argue, I have indulged in an argument to prove to myself that I can occasionally be brilliant. Suddenly I have the feeling that these problems are far beyond my scope. And yet, is it really that hard for me to understand the cure for the anxiety of bewilderment suggested to me by analysis—that is, to abandon quarrels of opinion and to go back to the source of life which is within me? To come back to myself instead of being "beside myself": off-center, scattered, and bewildered every time I am faced with the slightest outer prompting, for which I must elaborate a sane response in myself. To look inside myself, not from egotistic self-indulgence, but in order to fight against inner lies—the endless false justifications and excessive self-blame, the cause of all my mental distractions and wrong actions. If life is not first and foremost in social relationships, then I should find its meaning primarily within myself. This meaning is decided within me; it depends on my own decisions, my own volition, my mindfulness of secret intentions, too often distorted, my review of the motives that lead me to act. Is such a review really feasible? And can it possibly be based on a method and result in a technique of application?

This hypothesis is surprising—but only perhaps because it goes against my habitual thought patterns. Such a review is all the more amazing because I am starting to realize that it is leading me to a whole new vision of life, one which goes against all the accepted ideas and current ideologies. But what if this vision is actually a unifying one? What if it manages to dissolve the ambivalences and contradictions which inhibit my thoughts and actions? I who used to find it so difficult to regroup my wretched thoughts am now astonished to see that I can sit here and develop—admittedly with difficulty—the seeds of ideas which were planted in me during the analytic sessions. Although these ideas are not my own and have been transmitted to me, to the extent that they become guiding ideas and determining motives which heal my actions, will I not end up making them mine? Once I have integrated and digested them, will they not take on a life of their own? Will they not prove their fruitfulness and their potential for renewal by unfolding within me in accordance with their own structure, but enriched and subtly modulated by my own reflections and my own personality? If this was only a theoretical preoccupation, it would be quite ludicrous. However, it is clear to me that under the influence of these ideas I am already to some extent a different person from the excessively inhibited one I used to be. Could it be possible that I have entered into a path of healing? I hope so, but do not dare to believe it yet.

If I could one day say for sure that my hopes were not unfounded, I would be awe-struck to realize that this path had existed all along, unrecognized by the masses, and that I was lucky enough to stumble upon it. I am living the most amazing adventure. Nothing will ever prevent me from pursuing it.

The Big Dinner Party

I did it. I held a big dinner party at my place the other evening. I had such trouble making up my mind! Caught between my desire to play the socialite and throw a luxurious reception and the fear of its not working out, I was prey to my usual reflex of freezing in expectation without daring to do anything. Now, after the success, I feel somewhat queasy. I realize that I let myself be carried away with this extravagant reception for pretty dubious reasons—perhaps the desire to prove to myself that the cure has removed my inhibitions sufficiently for me to dare to expose myself. Obviously, the opinion of my social milieu still means a lot to me; I have suffered to much from the anxiety of being considered the squanderer of my family's material and moral heritage. An ostentatious reception could serve as a brilliant endorsement of my reconciliation with this caste, which had unanimously disowned and repudiated me after my "outrageous" marriage. It also provided an opportunity to let them know that I am gainfully employed, as befits a person of my extraction and standing. Proud of my newly won dignity, I even managed to forget for a moment the humiliations to which my alleged profession has exposed me and to convince myself that I have finally become my guests' equal. No doubt I must have been obsessed by many other motivations of this sort. I have a vague feeling that true disinhibition should overcome not only my obsessive anxiety, but also my desire to impress. By continuing to exhibit myself I will only fall into ever-greater absurdity. Still, I actually managed to assume my self-imposed role quite appropriately.

Or did I? Is it appropriate to indulge in playing the high-society snob in spite of my usually liberal ideas?

From the moment I started making up the guest list, I felt a sense of confusion and obsession. Now that I can relax and look back, I am beginning to see it more clearly.

I would have liked to invite only beautiful women and brilliant men. However, I had to not only take into account other priorities, like family ties and wealth, but also consider people I could hardly avoid inviting but who do not really appeal to me. How to bring together propriety and ostentation—idle urbanities, in which I inescapably get bogged down!

Then came the matter of setting the date! For me, scheduling anything in advance is a torture—I am always afraid of regretting it, afraid that by committing myself I will miss out on a much more attractive opportunity that will arise precisely that very same day! Another area of hesitation and perplexity involved choosing the menu, the wine, and the waiters. Everything I had learned to consider essential to the success of such an enterprise turned into almost unsurmountable problems because of my desire for perfection and my fear of failure. I was afraid of appearing stingy and mediocre or else seeming to flaunt luxury—which would not only be in very poor taste but would also occasion needless expense. I wanted the best in order to create an exceptional environment in which I could be the center of attraction. By deliberately letting everybody observe and criticize me, I had put myself into the type of situation I dread above all others.

However, my dinner was a big success. Everybody left late, delighted with the evening.

When everyone had gone and I was walking through the disorderly rooms turning off the lights, I caught myself thinking how well everything had worked out. I even asked myself why I should not repeat this sort of exploit from time to time. I started to laugh at the contrast between my present eagerness and my past anxieties.

It is not surprising that such a reception should spark off in me an agony of apprehensiveness at what people might say. As a bachelor, ceremonious receptions are far from being an obligation for me. I could have settled for something more informal, but my need to make a display was too strong.

Yes, it is my lack of self-esteem which is the root of my nervousness! Because I underestimate myself, I feel the need to win other people's esteem. A brilliant party is merely my chance to make up for the mediocrity of my character. Similarly, whenever I go on a date I always choose an excellent restaurant, fearful that my company might in itself not be exciting enough on account of my inhibited behavior. I also tend to sartorial elegance, displaying my upper-class snobbery and striking a pose to cover up my inadequacy.

It goes without saying that I invited Robert—my desire to display an external luxury which I know I cannot afford was naturally related in some way to my wish to cut him down to size.

Putting on a show, a tendency acquired as a small child, has now become a reflex. My lack of self-esteem seems to come from my parents' excessive demands and pressure, to which I could not respond satisfactorily as a child and which exposed me to constant scoldings, the expression of my parents' disappointment with me, of their low esteem for me. Certainly my parents loved my brothers and me very much, but the extremely rigid educational principles which were the standard during their generation made them take on severe, categorical, and rather dry attitudes. Not only did they consider expressions of affection to be "middle-class," they also disapproved of productions like this evening's dinner party. In addition, I was the second boy and may possibly have suffered at seeing how important the eldest male child was to my family; I may also have been jealous of the attention which my mother necessarily bestowed on my younger siblings and which I was no longer entitled to because of my age.

Left to his own devices, a child is helpless—he is totally in his parents' hands. It is easy to imagine that this situation, aggravated by jealousy toward my younger and elder siblings, could be the source of my more or less imaginary fear of not being valued by others and of my feeling of not deserving my lot in life. My parents' attitude, experienced as a denial of esteem, was absolutely agonizing. Can the feeling of security possibly develop in a child who does not feel an atmosphere of warmth, gentleness, and affection? Deprived of such an atmosphere, he feels a sense of abandonment, loneliness, even hostility. The origins of the child's nervous anguish can be found in the feeling of being denied his parents' esteem, against which he defends himself by accusingly, vainly, and sentimentally reasserting a bloated sense of his own self-worth.

Once he has acquired this habit in childhood, all his relations with others—society and the world—will quite likely be stamped with the fear of being underrated, accompanied by mistakenly defensive attitudes, the result of vanity, of mentally overestimating his worth. Yes, this evening's dinner party was merely a child's distorted attitude, an attempt to beg and buy others' esteem.

One of the main false problems I have created in my life is the need to win others' esteem, which necessarily makes me dependent on their opinions to an unsuspected degree. When vanity prevents me from claiming this esteem, all that is left to me is either moodiness or arrogance.

In an attempt to overcome my sullen arrogance I decided to open my doors to high-society splendors. I got carried away and threw the usual party. Now that it is over, I can reflect on my frivolousness and its distant causes, ever-present in the form of motivations.

How many times have I heard mothers tell their children, "You're such a naughty little boy! I don't love you anymore. Nobody loves disobedient children." Nor do these mothers love their children if they are lazy, cowardly, clumsy, noisy, dumb, tongue-tied, talkative, weak, pugnacious, or quiet. "Look at your friend: he's so nice! Why don't you follow his example? His mother must be lucky. If you behave yourself just like your friend, then. . . . " The poor child will obviously never be like his friend. He knows that he cannot be like his friend, yet he passionately wants his mother's admiration. "What can I do to be like other little boys who are loved by their moms?" That must be one of the roots of the endless, agonizing comparison with others that relentlessly pursues me.

It seems to me that children should be told when they have done something wrong or right, but they should never be made to doubt their parents' love. Would it not be better to make them feel that this educational scolding, often unavoidable, is one more expression of their parents' love? If parents create discomfort in their children instead of helping them adjust, their children will have feelings of inadequacy and want to be someone else. Not accepting themselves as they are, not using their own reality—of course imperfect but always improvable—as their point of departure, they run the risk of either abandoning in desperation any effort to adjust or inventing an ideal figure to imitate who is totally deserving of love. But since it is impossible to be completely free of fault, a child will always feel guilty of not achieving the ideal which is continually being set up for him to follow. This intolerable feeling of guilt can only drive him to look for a surrogate for his inner comfort—he will pretend to be the ideal character which his intensified desire for esteem has created.

Struggling hard to identify with this illusory figure,

his vain fantasies will condense into an obsessive project. Later, when he has grown up, the habit of vanity will still be there: he will be pursued by guilt in the form of the ideal he has dreamed up, thus prolonging his childish attitudes.

By consciously reconstructing a subconscious calculation based on mistaken feelings and meant from childhood on to satisfy at whatever price the need for esteem and affection, psychology has showed me that the origin of vanity lies in guilt. Vanity arises as a means to repress the excessive guilt, both unbearable and unavowable—the mistaken guilt which parents often produce in their children's minds through a love which lacks steadiness and understanding. It is parents who, because of their own distortion, are unconsciously responsible for this in the first place, even though the individual is entirely responsible for the wrong reactions arising from the propensities of his own nature. Parents are not the only ones to blame, since the blinders of wrong motivation are innate. The challenged child will turn into a challenger; yearning for love and esteem, he will tend to push his demand for affection too far. The fault of the nervous adult is to maintain this initial mistake instead of striving to overcome it; to superficially indulge in dodging the issue in his mind even though life is forcing reality on him as a corrective measure, punishing with a surfeit of suffering his attempts to escape into the vain comforts of fantasy.

Today, I am paying for this tendency toward self-indulgence acquired as a small child. I am paying for the mistake of having stayed stuck in an infantilism which has led to the excessive fear of not being accepted as I am. Overwhelmed by my parents' thoughtless scolding, I comforted myself by identifying with the imaginary character who haunted my dreams and reconciled me with myself, making any attempt to adjust seem unnecessary. Through my rebellious disobedience and my desperate inertia I was constantly producing precisely what I was most afraid of: the disapproval not only of my parents but, in the long run, of everybody else.

Thus, even today, I am still not quite able to accept myself as I am. My parents' disapproval has created in me an attitude of obsessive self-blame, continually transformed through repression into vain self-satisfaction. I cannot stand the reality of my shortcomings, but I refuse to develop my good points. Not having any esteem for myself, I do not deserve the esteem of others. What benefit can I get from vainly overestimating myself? This inflated self-image seems to be the basis for my continually disparaging others. However, my scornful disdain notwithstanding, since my vanity and guilt are the basis for my overrating myself, I am driven to listen to others' opinions constantly, on the lookout for signs that they might underrate me. As in all nervous individuals, my own self-contempt, overcompensated by my vanity, makes me fear that others may find me as contemptible as I myself secretly do. Maybe I will only be cured when I stop repressing my feelings of self-contempt, of guilt.

My exacerbated desire for others' approval and my exacerbated anxiety of their disapproval go hand in hand. They determine two forms of mistaken esteem, of wrongly evaluating all social situations and dealings with others. Needing others' esteem, the nervous individual on the one hand endeavors to display the good points he claims to have—and which he actually may have, but which he has not developed sufficiently; on the other, he is obliged to exert himself continually in view of camouflaging his real shortcomings. I either suffer for not being the ideal person or else I blame others for not taking me for the ideal. Refusing to show myself as I am, I try to act out the character I would like to be and end up looking like an actor overcome with stagefright.

I threw this party because I was set on showing myself off on stage and acting out my absurd role before spectators, who were to take this role for an ideal. I wanted to play the socialite who knows how to entertain lavishly; I would have been mortified if anybody had suspected that I am in fact a shy and anxious worrywart.

This nervous tangle will not stop growing as long as I make no effort to unravel it. In spite of their mental origins, my feelings with regard to my shyness, anxiousness, restlessness, and all my shortcomings have evolved into an obsessive psychological reality that determines my behavior down to the most minute details.

This false start in life, due to an inadequate education (i.e., to the wrong motivations which exist in both the parents and the child), makes one incapable of adjusting to the hardships, trials, successes, or misfortunes that life is constantly dealing out. Poverty, riches, sickness, fortuitous accidents, fortunate or unfortunate coincidences, all become occasions for failure and suffering, proof of the injustice of the external world. But this injustice, sometimes imagined and sometimes real, is counterbalanced by the implacable justice that rules one's inner world. There are actually no unsurmountable situations in life. Whether we are rich or poor, sick or healthy, good-looking or ugly, surrounded by people or alone, orphans or spoiled children, we can all be either happy or unhappy quite independently of external conditions, based only on our internal interpretations. If this was not the case, why would I, a relatively good-looking man, sound in body and fairly rich (extremely wealthy, actually, compared with most people)—a man of "high birth"—not be perfectly happy?

The acute anxiety I suffer from in the situations that fall to my lot is due precisely to my feeling of not being able to overcome these situations. But the life that has been given to us demands only that we achieve self-control in order to master circumstances and the difficulties they involve. By achieving independence, no matter how relative, with regard to external events, we can remain steadfast and balanced in the face of whatever happens—i.e., we can genuinely overcome accidental situations instead of vainly imaging we do. Life demands this attitude, since it punishes with suffering those who are not able to subdue its inescapable dangers. Overcoming the complications of existence is thus the essential task of human beings, and to the extent that we either carry out or neglect this task we are rewarded with joy or punished with anxiety and morbid suffering. Might not the guilt and self-blame experienced by inadequate individuals prove that, their vain justifications notwithstanding, they actually do feel life's immanent justice? Its secret reign is borne out by the fact that the tendency to repress guilt's warning, which is vanity, becomes an inexhaustible spring from which gush forth all the mistaken reactions which are the cause of the distress the nervous individual complains about.

My most unquestionable—and also most mysterious —reality is the fact that I am alive. Surely I should know how to live my life, this life that has been given to me? My agony, in fact, comes from not knowing how to live my life in a masterly manner; it seems that life demands that one should master one's desires, since it burdens all shortcomings with guilt. By punishing me in this way, life is warning me that I have made a wrong turn. The punishment—guilt dissatisfaction—is simultaneously a beneficial warning, since it tells me that I have strayed from the path of sanity that leads to joyful harmony with myself: the harmony of desires, the opposite of guilty anxiety. Thus, it is only up to me to discover my mistake.

The freedom which life gives me is this latent possibility of always being able to review my judgments immediately and thus change my behavior. This possibility of liberation is the most perfect justice. In fact, since it is intimately tied in with more or less intense guilt feelings, it is totally adjusted to each individual's sensitivity, whether crude or delicate, coarse or subtle, intelligent or narrow-minded. Each successive level achieved by the individual is matched by a superior level of harmony, and the effort to achieve it is an inexhaustible source of essential inner satisfaction. This inner success—that is, psychological balance—must surely be the best guarantee of social success, in accordance with one's capabilities and the demands of the actual situation.

To come back to the grand reception which triggered this chain of thought, I must add after all that it helped me uncover even more the source of my anxious disharmony. Instead of acting according to my own judgment, I split into two personalities: one who wants to put up a front and the other who is afraid of giving himself away. This excruciating split is the punishment for vanity's mistake. I thus find myself victimized by the slightest event, for instance the project of organizing a dinner party given out of the desire for extravagance and ostentation. It is amazing to see how entertaining can turn into an ordeal, a torment. What will happen the day that I am faced with a true test which I will not be able to shy away from?

Am I exaggerating? Of course! And that is precisely my sickness.

Exaggeration, no matter how imaginative, has real psychological consequences, which manifest as morbid suffering. Everything becomes understandable when one thinks that the slightest event throws the nervous individual's entire past behavior into question and triggers a chain reaction of guilt, an all-pervasive anxiety with regard to his future. The element of truth, in spite of the exaggeration, is that the slightest difficulty that arises in any situation—no matter how trivial—calls back the memory of all the unsurmounted difficulties of the past, charging the present with morbid shame and the future with inhibiting anxiety.

Having accepted me in its bosom, life demands of me that I be able to maintain myself in it satisfactorily—otherwise, how can I avoid dealing with the question of what I am doing in this world? This question undeniably expresses the anguish of feeling out of place in the world and the despair of seeing oneself excluded like an unwanted stranger. At home, as a small child, I remember feeling like an intruder who had not asked to be born. However, since I have after all been born, life demands of me—in the quest for essential satisfaction—only one thing: that I become myself. In other words, and this is something I must always come back to, to overcome my shortcomings and develop my good points.

To the extent that my mind can grasp clearly the elements of life's essential problem, the fear of the unknown gradually gives way to a sense of appeasement, since understanding the problem in itself contains the practical means to resolve it.

« 8 »

Sentimental Complications

*W*e spent the weekend at the forest of Chantilly, walking through the trees and talking. By constantly referring to couples she knows or to men who court her, Geneviève managed as usual to make me feel that I do not love her enough.

The results were disastrous. Her hints fixated my irritated attention. For all her efforts to reassure me by feigning to expect nothing from me, I froze into silent hostility, mulling over the idea of telling her openly that there is no possible future for us as a couple. The atmosphere was heavy with unexpressed thoughts, and we did not achieve a semblance of understanding until the evening, when we once again joined in bodily pleasures. These took on an importance that was far too exclusive, without however managing to dispel our ill-feelings. The lack of tenderness, of warmth, of spontaneous gentleness transformed our union into vulgar, animal-like coition.

Like me, Geneviève feels a certain guilt, which in part explains her demand that I love and appreciate her more. Yet her constant sentimental invitations make me feel very strongly that if I gave in to them, they would know no bounds. Her need to be appreciated would not diminish if I were to give her the ultimate proof, marriage. Would she not at that point want to be comforted for all her past hardships? And how could I possibly satiate such overflowing emotionalism?

Until now, she had seemed quite balanced to me. She had told me several times about the painful events she lived through during the war, the invasion of her country, the death of her parents, the loss of her possessions, her way of dealing with a thousand and one problems in the middle of a family that was going crazy, her feeling of abandonment when she finally found herself back in France with her child. I admired her courage in dealing with her responsibilities and enjoyed imagining that her languidness might be her way of cheerfully accepting her ruin.

She is in fact no less nervous than I. I had never realized it until now, since I tend to feel that all forms of nervousness are like mine and take the form of apathy. Geneviève is active and energetic and knows how to make decisions. These qualities are very apparent in her and impress me all the more because I am especially lacking in them. But her grasping, overeager desire to drag me into her emotional demands, some episodes she has recounted of a previous relationship with a man who, for all his charm, nonetheless submitted her to the most extreme humiliations, as well as her exaggerated sacrifices, seem to me now very revealing traits of a certain form of nervousness.

She is always expecting me to shower all kinds of tokens of affection on her: flowers, phone calls, and the like. She is obsessed with loneliness, which envelops her like a lead blanket. By nature very voluptuous, her imagination is haunted by sensual pleasures. Yet her childhood was bare of any form of enjoyment. She was married very young and more or less against her will to a handsome man, a rough and puritanical career officer whose brutal approach she experienced as a sort of rape. The horrible imprint that this event left in her mind closed her off for a long time to all forms of sensuality. Much later, her senses were once again aroused in the experienced arms of a charming but aging lover, whose caresses and thoughtfulness got the better of her marital fidelity. This situation culminated in a violent scene when, out of a need for frankness and honesty, she had both lovers confront each other. Her husband walked out on her, leaving her with her child. She was fascinated by her lover's impassioned pledges and believed that his kindness and attentiveness were proofs of his love. He had said that his marriage was unhappy, and she was taken in when he told her that he would divorce his wife and marry her. Deluded for years, she fought against her growing disenchantment. She was finally forced to acknowledge the deceitfulness and mythomania of the man, to whom she nevertheless felt strongly attached. She went through the most humiliating situations, but a caress, a small gift, a sweet letter, was enough to dispel the clouds. He knew how to hold her spellbound with the bedroom atmosphere which enthralled her, since she had so far only known the rugged approach of a husband who was severe due to his puritanical education and thoughtless due to his ignorance—and perhaps, deep down, his shyness. Geneviève did not really want to see through the equivocation that lay behind her lover's apparent fervor. But when, in spite of the exhilarating atmosphere, she finally faced the facts, she realized she had to break up with him.

For a long time, she was in a state of utter despondency and claims that only her daughter's presence prevented her from committing suicide. Nevertheless, she remembers this man with a mixture of tenderness and disgust. Listening to the way she praises this seducer's unique charm, I am inclined to think that she exaggerates his power in order to excuse her own weakness with respect to him and to smother her guilt with respect to a husband whose crudeness she focuses on too exclusively. Might she not also be exaggerating the deceitfulness of her former lover the better to play the victim's role? Still, I hesitate to believe it, because the same excessive love which excused her divorce made her too indulgent with regard to this man, for whose sake she had sacrificed her entire Catholic upbringing.

To escape from a past paved with the ruins of her family, her love life, and her wealth, Geneviève indulges in the exalted role of the self-sacrificing woman. She takes her misfortunes cheerfully and relies on her sweetness, selflessness, force, and courage to get her through, but her goodness of heart is contingent upon the strength that emanates from a great love. She relives her unrequited love and sets the stage for a new disappointment through the burdensome gift of her overflowing feelings and aching heart. I am convinced that she likes the role of the woman in love and sees men primarily as actors who can give her her cue. Whether they deserve her esteem or not is beyond the scope of her blindly emotional judgment—she seeks only the illusion of loving and being loved.

I do not mean to say that she only pretends to be gentle, brave, and generous: she actually does possess all these qualities. But she reflects herself too much in them: her vanity has been grafted onto these qualities.

If I was not a nervous person myself, Geneviève's vanity might not be as upsetting. Without an unbalanced partner to rebound on, her emotional reactions would decrease. If I was more easygoing and could respond to her behavior with a good-natured nudge, she would probably play along with me; however, being the way I am, her behavior only heightens my nervousness, which in turn arouses hers.

Understanding the process, I tried not to get upset at her for acting cute and made an effort to laugh off her voracious appetite for compliments and love tokens, but my words and actions betrayed my inner discomfort. My gestures were anything but light-hearted and carefree, and my jokes tended to express irony rather than humor. All that was left for me to was to attempt to explain my feelings, but this graveness, the opposite of the light-hearted banter I had aimed for, was the worst attitude I could have taken. I thought I was doing the right thing, but just try to answer feelings with reasoning! The effect was disastrous: in an instant I had become in her eyes a callous, selfish, cold-hearted, inhuman block of ice who cared for nothing but sex! She would even have felt contempt for me if her generosity had not aroused her pity. As could be expected, she concluded by adding that instead of self-indulgently getting all worked up over mind-deadening "psychological theories," I would be a million times better off to open up to more generous feelings and to take refuge in her arms. "Believe me, I don't want you to go through the same horrendous ordeals as I, but you really do deserve to fall into the clutches of a bitch who would make you understand all that you stand to lose if you lose me."

Her lecture sparked in me a reaction as nervous as my previous attempt at explaining: I was hurt at being judged so insensitive, outraged at her assumption that I have always been spared suffering, annoyed at her suggestion that psychology is mere theory. I was overwhelmed by an inexorable feeling of impotent rage. I became moody and barely answered her questions, since words felt totally useless. Then I started laughing. But instead of conveying good humor and cheerfulness, my sarcastic laughter implied: "You're too stupid! There's nothing doing . . . you'll never understand." Of course this attitude of accusatory superiority concealed not only guilt at not being able to open up straightforwardly, but also self-pity and despair about myself. This painful and strained attitude comes from certain obsessive intentions which unite me with Geneviève in spite of all our divergences, for deep down I agree with her: like her I feel that emotionalism is the only means to overcome the secret guilt I feel about sex, to me a form of bestiality. The only difference between us is that for her every man is capable of becoming the object of her idealization as long as he plays into her game, whereas for me no real woman can ever be as good as my imaginary idol. This secret agreement with Geneviève makes me see things her way and immediately exaggerates the element of truth contained in her aversion to my abusive and mindless use of psychology, which saps all its power to convince. Her accusation gives me the feeling of being insane, a nut case who latches onto a particular theory in order to hide his inadequacy under the relatively flattering mask of profundity. When you come right down to it, by advancing a theory whose truth I had not really experienced, I was in fact being an impostor. Although Geneviève's refutations had no bearing on psychology itself, they did highlight my imposture, and my wounded vanity refused to acknowledge the shameful character of my attitude. I absolutely needed to either prove that I was right, or else to prove Geneviève's stupidity by heaping sarcasms on her—which was much easier than explaining the feelings I do not have for her.

My emotional needs have actually transformed psychology from a means to achieve inner appeasement into an instrument of domination. My explanations (knee-jerk reactions born of vanity) are merely a screen to hide my inability to be carefree and good-humored.

If I was able to use it correctly, psychology would help me see through my own and Geneviève's wrong attitudes. It would help me understand that there are only two sane solutions available to me: either to acknowledge my supposed lack of feelings as a reality and endeavor to understand my share of the responsibility better in order to improve my behavior; or else, if I am really unable to adapt to the situation, to recognize frankly that it would be preferable to break up with Geneviève—a sober-minded decision devoid of hostility, quite the opposite of a sudden impulse. My choice would thus become objective and reasonable. Understood in all its motivations, it would not be followed by regret.

Writing these lines in the calm of introspection, I feel a

certain amount of tenderness for Geneviève. I deeply regret that my attitude and hers should destroy our good understanding, knowing full well that if one of us was more even-tempered and good-humored, the other would follow. If I was to break up with her in a state of irritation, I would condemn myself to repeating in my future relationships the wrong attitudes of my present one. The way I am today, my chances of meeting a well-balanced woman are pretty slim, since women of this sort have the flair and the wisdom to shy away from unbalanced men. And, among unbalanced, nervous women, Geneviève's type is, after all, one of the least obnoxious. If only I could get closer to the objective state I am experiencing right now, in spite of the heaviness of our relationship, there would still be hope that we could get along quite well. Instead of being considered reasons for despair, difficulties could be seen as trials which are ultimately positive since, if we deal with them in a clear-headed frame of mind, they can be used to develop a greater mastery over life. No matter what I do, there will be no dearth of difficulties in my present condition, since not only do I have to deal with the difficulties that life itself creates but also, nervous individual that I am, I am constantly manufacturing imaginary difficulties. I will never eliminate my nervousness totally, but I may hopefully manage to overcome my inability to reach a decision which is neither contradicted by regret nor inhibited by shame. Who knows? The day I am able to break up with Geneviève without excessive emotionalism might also be the day on which I can live with her without excessive irritation. . . .

« 9 »

Hesitations

I have just sat down at my desk, without much enthusiasm, because I have nothing else to do . . . and because I had set aside this afternoon for this task. Because it is too late at this point to rearrange my schedule . . . Had I gone out, I would have roamed about aimlessly, haunted by an inner voice that would blame me for wasting my time, for neglecting my notebook, for leaving Robert alone at Dictio.

You know what I feel like, rummaging around in my mind and writing everything down? A rag-picker combing through a garbage can.

Am I taking myself too seriously, perhaps? Do I take myself for a philosopher, I who have never been good at anything, whose academic career seems in retrospect to be a feat of faltering equilibrium? Year after year I was among the worst students, always threatened with being left back. Or is this a new infatuation, much like my flings of the past with astrology and theosophy, speculations not altogether devoid of interest but which proved disappointing on account of their unbearable extravagance? Am I sick to the extent of not being able to live without moral drugs and psychological purges? Am I a sluggish, diminished, abnormal being who can only be kept alive artificially? Suddenly, this room feels like a hospital ward and I am one of those miserable souls imprisoned in an iron lung, condemned to contemplate the ceiling eternally. But am I not being too scrupulous in the use of drugs and purges?

My psychologist has advised me not to torture myself, not to dissect my every action, to observe myself only in order to either dissolve my imaginative obsessions or else recover my balance after losing it and get over a state of emotional instability.

I am certainly interested in what I write; in fact, at this point, bent over my notebook, I have forgotten my initial resistance to sitting down at my desk. I feel liberated from my inner heaviness and weariness, my feeling of "What's the use?" The influence of this gloomy atmosphere is being dispelled precisely because the effort to articulate it helps me to understand it. Yet I still have the nagging feeling of being here only because I am unable to be in the mainstream of life!

I know that my resistance has manifested all throughout the therapy. I can quite easily see the anguish which, in some cases, I feel with respect to an awkward intervention on the analyst's part or the lack of power of conviction in his method—a weakness which no one can detect with greater sensitivity that a mentally ill person. As far as I am concerned, I feel attached to the cure out of a conviction which is reinforced with each session. Whenever I feel a flicker of resistance, I know it can only be due to my psychopathic state, which opposes the effort to be healed—that is, to a profound despair with respect to myself, which has always inhibited my efforts and which tends to make me back out too easily from the decisive effort required by the cure.

The thing I hold against psychology in these moments of weariness, when the feeling of being excluded from life fills me with all-pervading anxiety and despair, is that it has not cured me with one touch of its magic wand but has instead demanded patient effort. When it comes to that, I tend to feel that all my present activity is just a sinister joke, a blackmail of hope, a fraud as implausible as the promise to bring a dead person back to life.

Is it perhaps the inability to admit frankly to myself that I am the victim of a hope which leads nowhere that is chaining me to this table in spite of my desire to escape?

I am quite aware that the whole issue of my sickness and my hope of being cured are concentrated in this one question. An agonizing restlessness pursues me and will not relent until I manage to grasp clearly the true reasons for my alternating support and resistance.

Might it perhaps be a matter of putting order into the vast number of wrong motives which could have a bearing on my overzealous advocacy or my inhibiting resistance? Does not psychology teach me that, when I do this, the entire retinue of wrong motives will necessarily unfold within the framework of vanity versus guilt, accusation versus self-pity?

Both my support and my resistance, inasmuch as their motivations are wrong, must have aspects of vanity, guilt, accusation, and self-pity. And all these aspects must cover the three main areas of life: spirituality, materiality, sexuality.

Only by highlighting the wrong motives which underlie this contradictory straitjacket of overzealous compliance versus inhibiting resistance will I be able to find a practical solution to the problem of ambivalence and reach a unifying decision which will be either total support with all my being or else total detachment from the cure.

What seems obvious is that no other form of cure could arouse such contradictory feelings with such intensity. Unlike orthodox psychoanalysis, the study of motivations does not enjoy a more or less established public recognition. It can only rely on the authority conferred upon it by experience and the feeling of greater well-being that comes from experience. Admittedly, I can imagine that the psychoanalytic theory of pansexuality arouses doubts which can turn into resistance, but this resistance will be somewhat stifled by the theory's fame.

Since the search for motivation, on the other hand, does not benefit from a public recognition which is as crushing as it is reassuring, it leaves the patient only with the security of his own judgment and appeals only to his genuineness.

Perhaps it is this complication, due more to the present state of things than to the intrinsic nature of this type of treatment, that explains both my inordinate support and my agonizing hesitation.

How exhilarating to feel—or at least imagine—that I am one of the few who can understand this. Perhaps my constant self-complacency taints my support of the treatment with the myriad vanities which I can feel crawling around inside me during moments of greater insight.

On top of the vanity of feeling somewhat of a pioneer, I harbor the secret hope of one day achieving a competency which is denied to me in most areas. This competency, however, would lead less to a cure than to idle daydreams of authority and superiority aimed at fulfilling my immoderate fantasies. Am I really sure that, deep down, I do not nourish the hope of one day being able to write something other than a diary in the field of psychology? Perhaps it is precisely such absurd motives which, by contaminating my support of psychology, turn it into something obsessive and onerous.

Do I not have to pay an exorbitant price for all my vanities?

Triumphant vanity and the morose accusation of others for their lack of understanding automatically turn into their perverted opposite: triumph turns into submission and fear of others' opinions; accusation of others turns into guilty self-accusation and the obsessive feeling that I am constantly being watched, judged, condemned, and ridiculed by everyone in my effort at self-analysis. I know it because I have experienced it—I cannot possibly deny that this gamut of feelings actually exists within me.

These fears seep into my apathetic resistance, stimulating it to such a degree that my writing and the discipline it implies seem to me like the efforts of a pretentious visionary, a puffed-up fool.

But perhaps what I am really doing is transforming my struggle to be cured into a sinister farce. If the effort to achieve a more thorough understanding is turned into a vain triumph, it becomes not only meaningless but ridiculous. At that point, my fear of others' opinions, my dread of feeling isolated, and my lack of genuineness turn my suspicions against psychology and I try to justify myself by accusing psychology of being mistaken, of being the cause of my present torments.

My wounded vanity's objection to the treatment is actually only a reflection of my sickness, a need for my vanity to triumph even over psychology by depreciating it. This two-faced vanity—humiliated and triumphant—determines everything in my apathetic condition, including my disproportionate resistance and my inhibited support. Wavering between support and resistance is only a special case of inhibited exaggeration versus exaggerated inhibition, the law of ambivalence which governs all states of unhealthy psychological functioning.

Wrong motivation, the cause for my inhibited exaggeration with regard to everything, including psychology, is transferred from this pseudo-spiritual plane to all other areas of life, to the sexual and material planes, filling them in turn with wrong values and generalized ambivalence.

My excessive support of psychology, as long as it is due to the need for vain profit, inhibits me in my professional obligations. I accuse Dictio of being no more than a degrading hindrance. I bemoan not being able to free myself from it and give my all to psychology. Likewise, whenever I feel negative about psychology, I usually feel increasingly supportive or Dictio. I blame myself for not devoting myself entirely to a profession whose seductive promises of material profit invade my imagination at that point. It's a question of money, or course—but also much more, since I have turned my work at Dictio into a test of efficiency (which makes it not only obsessive but also unbearable). Here again my apathetic resistance and my hesitant support crop up, overlain with spurious meanings.

These same relations of ambivalence can perhaps be observed just as easily in the sexual realm. Just as by over-reacting I turn psychology into an unreal phantasmagoria, in the same way, whenever I put women on pedestals with my extreme sentimentality or degrade them into prey for my adventures with my extreme greed, they cease to be any-thing but the terrifying phantoms of a nervous individual's exacerbated and inhibited infatuation.

The inexorable law of reversals, whereby such miscal-culated satisfactions turn into dissatisfactions, can be ob-served everywhere. Mind, with its tendency to wrong evaluations, alternatively underrates and overrates material and sexual desires. Although this inexorability is disastrous as long as one subjects oneself subconsciously and obsessively to it, understanding it gives one the power to anticipate the vast-ness of its psychopathic consequences. Only insight into one's perverted patterns, which extend by analogy to all areas of life, gives one an inkling that a more wholesome path is possible. And this insight can only be the exact opposite of morbid and inhibiting overexcitement. Overexcitement is merely the caricature of cool-headed enthusiasm with its harmonizing force. This enthusiasm also has the power to as-sert the value of things, something it is able to extend to all aspects of life including sexual and material desires, espe-cially if it is guided and sharpened by insight into the truth. If I fight back every day the temptations of overexcitement which pervert my desires, if I oppose these temptations, not in a moralistic way, but by anticipating their false promises of satisfaction, my impulses can gradually recover their own strength, the force of enthusiasm.

This inexorable law, extending itself through analogy, applies both to the causes of the deformation of one's character and to the causes of its reformation. I have just understood that enthusiasm (the opposite of inhibiting overexcitement) is nothing other than joy (the opposite of anxiety in all its forms, particularly anxious guilt).

If this is the case, it stands to reason that the only way to grasp the inexorable law of these healthy versus unhealthy analogical relationships is by lucidly releasing one's guilt, through the enthusiasm of going ever deeper until true analysis is condensed into true synthesis—the joy of knowing and, most of all, the joy of self-knowledge. Only this release can lead to genuine thought and consequently to genuine spontaneity in real, active life.

I am starting to see the core of the problem that hems me in: an underlying wrong idea about spontaneity. Since spontaneity for most people is synonymous with casualness, it tends to manifest in activities devoid of sane orientation and conditioned by current ideas. But this wrong, trite idea of spontaneity is in fact only a falsely justifying motivation, a wrong evaluation, leading to a downward path: the easy way out of never taking a closer look at things, which determines the pseudo-spiritual mania of looking for the meaning of life in the unleashing of sexual and material desires. True spontaneity is perhaps to be found only in sanely oriented activities, developed with genuineness and based on relating to one's own thoughts; this might be the only way to share in a common truth.

The project to achieve liberating insight may be the sanest and most important one that mind can undertake in its search for the satisfaction of truth, a satisfaction peculiar to mind, which can be attained only through the discipline of thorough elucidation. This is in fact the case, since consciousness, as long as it is unable to understand the secret progress of motivations, will always be partially blind and therefore subject to the suggestive power of current opinions.

People with such conventional views will always prefer sexual adventures and material employment of the most lucrative and prestigious sort to the efforts of mind. Whenever I lapse into current opinions, I get caught up in an obsessive need for approval which makes me dependent on others. At that point, my fears of exposing myself to their irony leads me to discredit psychology—a pretext which opens the way for my fears to oppose my present efforts at elucidation and deeper insight.

This inner discord gives rise to the obsessive counterproject (ambivalent with respect to my tendency to be ironical about myself) of clinging to the supposedly curative analytical process. I thus throw myself into it with a convulsive frenzy which robs it of its value, its impulse, its enthusiasm, and its joy.

Dissatisfied with my psychological preoccupations, which I myself have thus rendered ineffective, I rebel against my overzealous support. My resistance tells me I should break away from psychology, but I am haunted by one last question: "Do I have the courage to say no to the analyst, who for me embodies psychology?" I end up blaming myself for not doing it, imagining that my only obstacle is my fear of actually having to take a step.

If I was to let myself get caught up in these traps, my vanity would finally submit to my desperate resistance and blow up a temporary loss of heart into a definitive escape, fancifully transmuting my cowardice into a brilliant proof of my courage.

But it is precisely the cure which, as long as I keep on an even keel, might enable me to no longer be buffeted around by my weakness and cowardice—i.e., my anxieties and their vain justifications.

I have reached a turning point in the analysis of my resistance—I am now starting to cast off its spell.

What a sense of freedom! I can only attribute it to my sharp insight into the ins and outs of the problem, my distorted motives and the wrong reactions they lead me to.

I have just realized that, had I forced myself to say no, I would have been giving in to the most dangerous temptation of all: my habitual tendency to short-circuit any process which would have led me this time to my final ruin.

If I had yielded to my desire to give up, I would actually have been giving up on myself. I would finally have managed to transform my imaginative despair into real despair —for good.

« 10 »
The Dream

*L*ast night's dream gave concrete form to yesterday's reflections. Deciphering it with the analyst during the
session has given me insight into a basic misconception
which is opposing any further progress.

This misconception concerns a global view resulting
from the study of motivations and leading to a theory of
guiding values, of sublimatory motivations for activity.

By extrapolating the analytic experience of the cure, I
can glimpse a possible synthesis, which must necessarily be
summed up in a theory. It is this process of achieving deeper
insight that I stumble over and occasionally rise up against.

Yet is it not a peculiarity of human beings to reflect on
life and its meaning? The method I am following has allowed me to catch a glimpse of the essential truth which is
originally condensed, the world over, in the enigmatic language of myths, collective dreams which are the foundations of culture.

I confess that I do not feel familiar enough with this
field of study to delve into it here. I am both somewhat
stunned and deeply struck by the unaccustomed suggestion
that the combats of mythical heroes might symbolize the
intimate struggles of the human soul: the conflicts between
right and wrong motivations, between sanity and insanity.
The meaning of life, anticipated by mythical wisdom,
would thus be to overcome on the one hand devouring

monsters, symbols of the often monstrously exacerbated desires that devour us, and on the other the demons that
inhabit us, symbols of the justifications born of our vanity.

Could it be that good and evil, sanity and insanity—
the value and lack of value of each individual and of the
whole of existence—are developed within us? Must one
admit, as this method of deciphering suggests, that sane and
insane solutions are expressed, down to their most minute
detail, in the symbolic language of mythical wisdom?

Could it be that this essential truth has existed, enig-
matically veiled, since the beginning of time? In this case,
the important thing would be to unveil it in order to make it
accessible to our intelligence. I am deeply convinced that it
is not a purely theoretical issue. Besides, my analyst is constantly demonstrating the practical scope of this truth to
me. According to him, not only myths—collective
dreams—use symbols to denounce the strayings of mind, its
false motivations: enigmatic symbols are still alive in us,
right now. Symbolic expression would thus underlie the
structure of every possible illogical manifestation from
which human beings suffer, including obsessions, hallucinations, and delusions. But the greatest surprise of all is to
realize that the meaningful symbol of myths is also the basis
for the imagery of my night dreams! Deciphering them
during my analytic sessions has often shown me that dreams
are not only a continuation of daydreams, but also contain a
warning with regard to the perniciousness of daydreams.
My dreams are an extension of the unfinished deliberations
of my waking state. Their symbolic imagery reflects my innermost conflicts. Dreams symbolically announce the
motives which, unknown to me, condition my inadequate
actions. Translating my dreams into conceptual language
helps me release my secret intentions, subjecting them to review and self-control.

This viewpoint, which unifies into a single whole all
of one's psychological activities including dream states, is

the ground both for deciphering symbolic language and for applying the healing technique, based on self-control in the waking state. This is due to the fact that my daydreams, the cause of my active deficiencies, revolve around the same conflicts as my night dreams. This therapy differs from the usual attempts to overcome conflicts by only tackling inadequate actions and by tackling them head-on. Such a project, as I have experienced so many times, leads only to a convulsive and moralizing effort, destined to collapse sooner or later as long as perverse motivations are left untouched. The liberating struggle—as demonstrated, incidentally, in myths and dreams—must take place at the level of my inner deliberations. Mistaken evaluations are the basis of wrong voluntary decisions and distorted actions; these can be combatted only by reasserting right values. The only sane way for me to deal with my misguided motives and misleading promises of satisfaction is to develop right ideas within myself and breathe life into them through conscientious reflection. Analysis can thus lead me to synthesis—a global vision of right ideas, which one could call guiding values. If the conflict is really between right and wrong evaluations, it follows that right values—true values—can be discovered as soon as our mind agrees to lift the cloak that conceals our strayings, our deceitful justifications.

When vain self-justification, our way of repressing guilt, reaches the advanced stages of blinding repression, it finds expression in symbolic language. This is what gives rise to the illogicality of psychopathic symptoms, all of which express in dream guise either repressive vanity or repressed guilt. But this same symbolic language is also used by myths and dreams to represent inner conflicts and their right or wrong solutions (this fact will never cease to amaze me, nor can I ever remind myself enough of it). Analytic technique thus reaches the deepest layers of the extraconscious. I am starting to realize that it constitutes a coherent whole.

The thoughts I have just articulated are based on the interpretation of a dream, whose explanation during the session revealed to me the extent to which, deep down, I still oppose therapeutic elucidation even when, in spite of my occasional reservations, I consciously take my support of therapy for granted. As has often been the case, understanding my dream will take me one step further toward gradually dissolving my resistance.

I will attempt to sum up the hidden meaning of this short, simple, and very revealing dream.

In the dream, I refused to accept from my tailor the delivery of a formal evening suit I had ordered, claiming that his price was exorbitant. In the end, I consented to receive from the tailor a fountain pen in lieu of the suit.

Interpretation here means introducing the motivations suggested by the images without neglecting any of the elements of the dream.

The evening suit I had ordered from the tailor symbolizes my wish to acquire an attitude that will enable me to flaunt myself in polite society and put on a good show. The person I am asking to "tailor" a made-to-measure suit for me is my analyst. Initially, my purpose for going into analysis was to throw off my inhibitions and become a great socialite who moves in fashionable circles. I would have been happy if the analysis had provided a costume for me: an external attitude, a disguise. This motive still seems to exist and to oppose my efforts to achieve greater insight as advised by my analyst—this is the "exorbitant price" which I refuse to pay. However, I accept to exchange my suit for a fountain pen. The pen symbolizes my attempts to achieve deeper understanding, my theoretical preoccupations, my writings—the act of writing this journal, which is making me spend my evenings glued to my desk instead of indulging in the pleasures of society. The suit I am giving up is actually much more expensive that the fountain pen I am getting in return.

The dream is a warning that, whether I am aware of it or not, society life is actually more important to me than taking a close look at myself. The analyst in whom I am consciously placing all my trust is here depreciated, degraded to the level of a tailor, who is cheating me to boot. My choice of the fountain pen is merely resignation underlain by rebellion.

However, I feel entitled to add that an isolated dream does not express one's entire psychological constellation but only one's present inclinations, which may very well be transient. As a continuation of our daytime deliberations, night dreams speak to us only of our present, improperly established motives, which we have repressed in our waking state. This does not exclude the possibility of our being driven also by other, more valid motives. Dreams express our guilt-ridden desires—in my case the desire to show off, the cause of my rebellion. The presence of guilt, even repressed guilt, seems to point to the presence of an essential need running counter to one's deficiencies, which takes on the role of assigning guilt. The insight which the analytic sessions have given me tells me that the aim of dreams is not to satisfy our repressed desires but, on the contrary, to warn us that, for our own good, we must endeavor to free ourselves from the repression which placed us in painful contradiction to ourselves.

As the dream I have recounted indicates, I had actually entered into analysis in the hope of throwing off the shackles of social inhibitions (of acquiring a tailor-made dress suit). But it is equally true that I had read the analyst's book on motivations before accepting the help of the cure. This book had struck me deeply, for I had felt that the analysis I was considering was a chance to delve deeply into myself, something I had always secretly longed for and which was much stronger than my desire to flaunt myself. I still remember both the yearning and the dread aroused in me by this opportunity to deepen my understanding.

Thus, it is hardly surprising that my initial ambivalence, attested to by numerous dreams, had maintained itself throughout the analysis and was finally manifesting as the central problem I must tackle.

The degree of success of the therapy will depend on the extent to which I manage to dissolve my basic ambivalence (my exacerbated desire for both deeper self-knowledge and dissipation).

Will I finally lean in the direction of disinhibiting my mind? Will I, of my own free will and without any hint of rebellious resignation, get to the point where I can fully accept the fountain pen—the effort to unmask myself—with the in-depth self-examination it requires? Will I prefer it to the masquerade, to my dressy outfit? Or will I go on contenting myself with partial disinhibition in order to enjoy my privileges without too much guilt? In this case, I would find myself drifting through life as a spectator, fairly aware of the process thanks to the knowledge I have acquired, observing both myself and the world with somewhat disillusioned irony, perhaps not completely without humor.

I consciously prefer to entertain the hope that I will mange to go beyond this project and, my temptations and resistance notwithstanding, achieve not only a more valid degree of recovery, but also one that is, for me, more satisfactory.

The analyst, I know, will leave the choice up to me. But the choice needs to ripen. Who am I in terms of my deepest tendencies? That seems to be the riddle formulated by the dream.

If I take a closer look at the dream, I may actually discover an invitation to find a saner solution—in spite of the present resistance that the dream expresses. I would like to believe this.

If I had casually rejected the pen, the implications of the dream would quite definitely have been negative, since this act would have indicated an underlying desire to end the analysis.

But I did accept the pen—therefore I do wish to go on deepening my self-knowledge. It is all a matter of knowing the motive which will make me stick to the analysis. The point here is less to translate the dream than to understand my state of mind better. The desire to go on with the analysis remains suspect because, as the dream suggests, it is underlain by a rebelliousness which degrades acceptance into resignation and timid submission. I know that I am capable of such a motivation, but I also know that I am capable of rebelling against myself and the weakness which the dream pointed out to me. The dream can be taken as a warning that I should revolt not against analysis but against my own weakness. Only such a stand could turn my submissive resignation into full acceptance. According to a constant rule, each figure of the dream is a symbol of a psychological attitude on the part of the dreamer. The tailor/analyst symbolizes my own vision of the cure and its possibilities of bringing about a fairly deep change in myself. Unless my own impetus suddenly takes a leap and defies the inertia of my submissive shyness, nothing could ever force me to give up my showy outfit, as I did semi-unwillingly in the dream. This deep-rooted drive is starting to wake up—with some pain, admittedly—from its discouragement and dormancy.

It seems that, deprived of healthy nourishment, this impulse lies dormant within us and grows lethargic and faint.

What could I have been looking for in my readings since my earliest childhood if not a sane orientation? Adventure, perhaps, with its unforeseen vicissitudes? Of course. But this superficial curiosity may have been a mere surrogate for an unsatisfied need to find a sane orientation, which excessively idealistic and moralistic conventions are unable to offer.

As a teenager, I looked forward to the life that awaited

me and searched for its meaning in fictional adventures. I was like a man parched with thirst, stumbling toward a mirage—I was lucky enough not to chance on stagnant waters to slake my thirst. Youth, ever eager to escape from the boredom of a conventionalized existence, is always looking for adventure, for the unexpected. How could I avoid being seduced by the cynicism of unleashed desires presented by a certain type of decadent literature, an expression of our generalized bewilderment?

In fact, all my past strayings rested upon the conflict of moralism versus amorality as it is reflected, without the hint of a solution, in today's literary production—the showy dress of a period of history which has lost the meaning of values. It was this bookish pseudo-culture which, to a great extent, had led me to founder in my neurosis of submissive revolt.

I may finally be starting to understand that the only existing remedy is to return to the sources of life.

Can one possibly imagine a more moving and unexpected turn of events than this renewal, which is enabling me to understand myself and my inner odyssey and inviting me to search for the image of my own fate in the world's most ancient and up-to-date adventure stories: myths and dreams?

My dream does actually bring me face to face with the problem of my life and suggests a sane solution. However, if I am to understand the meaning of this solution which the dream has wrapped in too much imagery and presented in a disguise far too symbolical, I must grasp it in a clearer, less enigmatic form. This renewal is not the quest for a new truth with regard to the meaning and value of life, but a new formulation of an unchanging truth. In order for this truth to guide me clearly and without confusion, I must formulate it conceptually, and I can only achieve this through a continuous effort to take a closer look at myself. Far from taking me away from ordinary life, this effort is the only way I can discover both the source of all understanding and the resources for a saner and more active life.

My writing (the fountain pen of my dream) is one of the many possible means of achieving greater insight which I could have chosen. I can abandon it, as long as I do not abandon the true means: the analysis of my deficiencies and their underlying motivations. Only analysis can help me reach the true goal: synthesis, a vision of guiding values. The dream pointed toward a danger which often looms before me: that of confusing my writings, at best a complementary tool, with the necessity for real, living experience. This confusion is the deep-seated cause for my overzealous advocacy of psychology and my devious resistance to it, for my submissiveness and rebelliousness. In pointing to this, the dream invites me to dispel the confusion by including it in the analysis of my motives. My writing only becomes a burdensome excess load when I no longer see it as a means for analysis but as an end in itself. At that point, it becomes a task of vanity, both obsessive and grueling—a showy outfit.

By deciphering the dream more thoroughly it is possible to broaden the meaning that can be derived at first sight. By condensing a twofold meaning into both the symbol "fountain pen" and the symbol "dress suit," the dream symbolizes the confused entanglement of wrong motivations. The fountain pen refers both to my personal effort at self-analysis by means of this diary as well as to the overall theory or vision of guiding values which the analyst is offering me. The dress suit represents both my desire for social disinhibition (which leads me into idle daydreams of trite and conventional licentiousness) and its ambivalent counterpole, its pseudo-spiritual travesty: my moralistic overemphasis on mind (the cause for my social inhibitions). The excessive hopes I place in keeping a diary—and, more generally, in pursuing my analysis—degrade my effort to be cured into a display of vanity. This prompts me to invest myself with extraordinary qualities, incites me to show off and strut about and leads me down the lazy path of over-excitement versus inhibition, of hoping against hope, of reluctant support versus rebellious resignation.

It is pen in hand that I have just understood my stray-ings and unraveled my distorted motives. My aspirations are all astir, telling me unanimously that I must accept the exchange proposed by the dream—for my own good and of my own free will; that I must choose the pen of deep reflection; and that the worst thing that could happen to me would be to resign myself to wearing the flashy outfit.

However—and I can never remind myself of this enough—the best aspirations do not necessarily lead to their fulfillment. They too are motives and, like all motives, succumb far too easily to the temptations of vanity. Assaulted by these temptations, aspirations may become mere pretexts, wishful thinking, pseudo-sublimations destined to fall apart. No matter how much truth might be contained in the broader analysis of the dream and its warning, the first-level interpretation nevertheless pointed to subconsciously obsessive revolt. There will inevitably be relapses before obsession gives way to a healthy aspiration. What other means do I have to find a sane way out of the conflict of motives than to continually resume the task of deepening my understanding (that is, to take up the pen again and again)? I can throw off the shackles of wrong evaluations condensed into obsessive temptations (the dress suit) only by lucidly actualizing myself and reasserting real values. Only thus can I gradually achieve freedom from the confused entanglement of wrong motives and from the obsessive temptation of false promises of satisfaction.

« I I »

Breaking Up

*L*ast Saturday afternoon, Geneviève invited me to spend the weekend at the country house of some friends of hers.

Our hosts' cottage lay above a sloped garden with a view over flat meadows. A winding row of poplars outlined the meanders of the stream we had crossed in the village. At several points, the stream had carved islands around the picturesque old mansions we had seen on our way. Slightly melancholy because of the evening fog, this lovely setting contrasted sharply with the drabness of the cottage, rented on a yearly basis. Our welcome, however, was quite warm, friendly, and heartfelt.

We were introduced to the other guests, some ten in number, in whose company we were to spend the weekend. Seeing as it was getting late, we went directly upstairs to our bedroom to get ready for dinner.

By the time the bell was rung for dinner, we were all mingling in the living room, sipping our drinks. The alcohol in our apéritifs had rapidly broken down our inhibitions and created a congenial atmosphere between people who, for the most part, had never met before. We were all in great spirits as we trooped into the dining room. Dinner was quite cheerful and noisy.

On returning to the living room, I started a conversation with a young woman, some twenty-five years old, pretty and quite bright. Geneviève came over to tell me that she was ready for bed. I said, "Fine, I'll be up in a few minutes." Half an hour later, on entering the bedroom, I immediately noticed Geneviève's annoyance. "In bed already? That was fast! All this chatter has exhausted me. She was quite nice and pretty, that young blonde I was talking to."

"You can go right back to her if that's what you want! You were certainly flirting up a storm, the two of you!"

I started laughing to calm her imagination and throw her off the scent. But she clung to her idea and accused me of having embarrassed her in public by neglecting her all evening, something "everyone had noticed." I maintained that such parties are specifically meant to separate couples temporarily, seeing as they have all the time in the world to gaze into each other's eyes. "Besides, you seemed to be having a great time too. Men were flocking around you."

"Precisely. That was George and his brother, who noticed that I was all alone and were kind enough to come over and keep me company."

I acknowledged that, stupidly enough, I am embarrassed to publicly show my feelings toward a woman with whom I am having a relationship, whereas I do not mind being friendly with a stranger whom I will probably never see again, since this does not arouse the sense of modesty which usually prevents me from expressing my feelings with people I know. I told her how sorry I was for this attitude which had upset her, but which nevertheless proved that she, and not one of the lady guests, was the woman I really liked.

I tried to pull Geneviève into my arms, but she withdrew further into her thoughts, claiming that I was ashamed of her, that she was probably not pretty enough for me. "Like all men, you're taken in by the first glittery little thing with nice legs that comes along!" Her criticism touched a sore spot: I actually do tend to let myself be seduced by any strange woman with nice legs who happens by and invest her in my imagination with the most exalted qualities. I felt all the more hurt because this little scene of jealousy was brutally highlighting an impression I had tried to push back into the shadows of semiconsciousness. I knew, without ever having clearly admitted it to myself, that Geneviève's beauty was in fact rather unspectacular and that her elegance was slightly outmoded. She was not a very flattering girlfriend to have in most people's eyes.

At this point I felt incapable of giving my troubled emotions a boost, too weary to make the effort to be nice. For a long while, we lay beside each other, sullen and resentful. She was leafing mechanically through a fashion magazine. Turning my back to the light, I lay still and tried to go to sleep. She turned off the light, but our irritation prevented us from falling asleep. We tossed and turned, caught between bodily desire and resentment. She put her hand on my chest. I drew closer, grateful that she had been the one to take the first step toward a reconciliation, something I did not feel up to since I was convinced that I was the injured party and felt that I had already reached out to her in every possible way.

I put my arm around her and placed my cheek against hers. In the dark, our lips brushed against each other. We embraced, but in spite of this outward show, our hearts were not in it.

The next morning, Geneviève woke up complaining —she had had a bad night, she had not slept very well. I, on the other hand, seeing that I was again in a situation of all-pervasive reluctance, hardly daring to speak of anything but the most commonplace subjects in the blankest tone of voice, wondered what the hell I could be doing there beside her. I was furious at not being able to escape from this embarrassment, at not being able to focus on the funny side of this mutual torment, which reminded me of the classic scene of two clowns wrestling, pulling each other apart, seemingly in great pain, not realizing that in their entanglement they are actually attacking their own limbs. Although I could recognize this mechanism in my own and Geneviève's behavior, I felt unable to disengage the gears, to break this ridiculous deadlock.

We spent the morning in our room. It seemed endless. We were secretly looking forward to being with the other guests and relaxing again. But the pleasure of lying in bed and the fear of waking up our hostess seemed to prevent us from going downstairs. Finally, the sound of congratulatory voices wafted up through the stairwell. It was almost noon. Whew!

After lunch we went for a stroll along the stream. We walked in groups of two or three, taking advantage of the occasional stops to reassemble in different combinations before slowly moving on with a fresh supply of laughter and small talk. I made an effort to talk to Geneviève, who also made an effort to answer, but we were still under the shadow of the previous evening's hostility.

Alone with each other on the way back to Paris, after exhausting the topic of our impressions about the people we had just left, we found we had nothing much to say to each other. Restful, comfortable silence may well be one of the charms of a good relationship, but in our state of antagonism we felt obliged to talk and cover up this deadly silence, pregnant with the accusations which we could almost hear grinding about in each other's mind—in our opponent's mind, I should say more crudely.

Home again! I stopped the car in front of Geneviève's building. I was hoping to leave right away to avoid prolonging this unbearable situation, but I also wanted to avoid upsetting Geneviève by seeming to be in too much of a hurry. I did not dare to get up and open the door for her, and no words came to my rescue. At long last, in a voice that refused to take on a proper intonation, I made this shrewd observation: "Well, so here we are." These wretched words seemed to quiver in their effort to break the heaviness of a silence charged with anxiety.

Finally she spoke: "It's getting late." Then, timidly: "I haven't prepared anything for dinner, but if you want to come up, we'll fix something."

At that point I finally blurted it all out: "Listen, Geneviève darling, I'm extremely fond of you, but we mustn't kid ourselves: we just don't get along! It's my fault, but also yours to some extent, or maybe it's nobody's fault, or all mine. . . . I don't know. But what I do know is that we've just spent two absolutely horrible days together. You're pretty, charming, intelligent, very attractive . . . but there's something in our personalities that pushes us apart. You object to my ideas—you say they pit us against each other. But what can I do? Right or wrong, that's the way I am! My theories seem stupid to you, but they're mine and I find them interesting. I believe in them, so what can you do about it? I haven't concealed my unbalance from you, and I know it sometimes makes me unpleasant. I make you suffer, and that's no good for you; and I'm going crazy myself. It's a real shame! But I can't change the situation by decree. I'm not the man you need, the man you long for. You need a nice, gentle, affectionate man. You've had a rough life. You've lost everything; all you have is your daughter, and you have to take care of her. I'm not at all the man who could create the home you and your child need. I can't ask you to put up with my moodiness, my peevishness. My theories about emotionalism offend you, but I'm not about to give them up. Don't you think it would be better if we broke up? You can be sure I'd miss you a lot—but the fondest physical attraction isn't enough to build a lasting relationship on."

Geneviève was crying. Awkwardly, I tried to calm her down. Between sobs she told me how hard it was for her to be alone, that all she wanted was a little bit of affection, that my harshness was not my true nature, that just one month ago she had been so happy.

I did not know what to answer, what to say. I looked for what might have been the best side of our relationship one month ago and could not find anything. I cradled her in my arms like a child. Her tears streamed down my cheeks, my fingers, my lips that caressed her damp eyes. She raised her eyes to mine—I felt her breath on my lips, her breasts in my hands. We were seized with a mad desire to embrace.

We stayed for a long time in each other's arms without talking. Finally, we had to part. I suggested that we go to the theater Thursday evening.

« 12 »

Ambivalences

I am still haunted by a sense of uneasiness with regard to the issue of my support of and resistance to the psychoanalytic process, even though I reflected upon it a few days back and deciphered the dream which condensed it. This is a sign that I have not resolved the underlying motivations sufficiently and should make an effort to gain an even greater insight into them.

After my effort to analyze it, however, the discomfort has taken on a new shape. I now seem to be experiencing its flip side: I cannot help being angry at myself for having taken a wrong turn. My ill humor is no longer directed against the analyst, but against myself. This emotionalism with regard to the analysis which I had devalued has led me to excessive self-accusation. In fact, this reverse guilt may be no more than another of vanity's attempts to overreact.

What I really seem to be blaming myself for is not being up to the situation, not being able to understand the value of self-analysis in terms of my own experience. Although I cling to the analysis desperately, I am constantly being gnawed by doubts, and even by the temptation to reject it—which is exactly what the vast majority of people would do, for all my smugness in disparaging their understanding.

What is at stake is no longer the value of psychology per se, but my own value. No matter which way I turn, I am faced with doubts about my own self-worth, which are in turn related to my anguish at other people's opinions. If the theory I support in the hope of being cured turns out to be worthless, I am no more than a fool; but if, without further investigation, I oppose a system of thought whose cohesiveness I cannot deny, I will remain forever in the trivial ignorance I disapprove of. And, to top it all, I would lose all hope of being cured.

What I now blame myself for excessively is the fact that my doubts have turned into resistance. When all is said and done, why should it be wrong to doubt? Doubt is a stimulant for elucidation. The real dangers are sterile skepticism or facile belief; like Scylla and Charybdis, they are the two perils I must avoid.

The overemphasis involved means that both the gullible yes and the skeptical no to which I have been prey so far have exactly the same fallacious meaning. They lead me to flip back and forth between moments of overzealous inspiration and relapses into doubt. The gullible yes in which I am presently taking refuge in my state of excessive self-blame will only prepare the ground for a relapse into skeptical doubt.

This alternation is no more than a special case of the law of ambivalence. It arises initially on the level of motivating deliberations, ultimately invading every activity with its emotional disturbance. To want and at the same time not want—this is the law that governs those who are simultaneously high-strung and low-key, both credulous and skeptical with respect to everything. I could actually use the expression "mental illness,"—that is, "illness of mind"—to designate this feeling of general discomfort I suffer from, this all-pervasive emotion that grips me whenever I am with a group of people and prevents my brain from operating sanely, this inability to make lucid judgments whenever I am under the shock of meeting another human being.

On the other hand, away from such restrictive situations, in the solitude of my reflections, I am now able at least to consider things calmly, instead of wasting my time mulling over them as I used to do.

This is a sign of progress that makes me hope that I will gradually learn to maintain my composure even in my social relationships, in my active life. The fact remains that the positive results of my solitary reflections have not yet sufficiently congealed into a new attitude, into an active reflex. Faced with another human being, I far too often—not always, but quite frequently—become engrossed in all-consuming ruminations, heightened by my feelings of superiority/inferiority. The immediate demands of the situation may leave no room for thinking things over, yet my attention is continually captured by the effort to remember, one by one, the results of my previous private reflections. This results in a sort of confused mixture of the reflexive and active states. Even though both states are necessary, the important point is to separate them clearly so that in the final analysis they can interact sanely.

I should attempt first to achieve relative freedom in the solitude of my reflections, outside restrictive situations. Private reflections are not an end in themselves, although they are a means to achieving sane activity, something I cannot do if I force myself to withdraw excessively from the world. It is essential not to run away from active life, for in order to experience the morbid effects of this emotional invasion through self-observation, there must first be an alarm signal in the form of an aggressive reaction on somebody else's part or a deficiency in my own activity.

Only active deficiencies which I acknowledge to be alarming instead of wrongly justifying them are able to prevent my imagination from vainly brooding over my exacerbated hopes and inhibiting anxieties. However, if I do not want the anticipation of failure to push me deeper into anguish, I need an analytic tool which can point out within myself the hidden causes of my active deficiencies; that is, wrong motives and their misleading promises of satisfaction. This tool is psychological calculation. Its precision comes from the fact that it relies on the study of the ambivalent split which, by oscillating between overexcitement and inhibition, degrades my healthy feelings into contradictory ill-feelings, that is, resentments. By using this calculation knowingly and carrying it over to the conscious plane should enable me from now on to unmask the games of ambivalence which, although morbid, nevertheless obey a psychological law, as well as to find my bearings in the subconscious maze in which the thinking mind goes astray and loses its way as long as it remains blinded by emotion. By clarifying the deceitful subtleties of psychological calculations born of vanity, I should be able to give rise to cautious psychological calculation, the genuine tool provided by the science of motivations for clearing away the quicksands of emotionality and bringing to light the solid bedrock of lucid reasoning and the effort to discover sane values.

I have observed that the troubles which plague my initial efforts at self-analysis and which make the whole endeavor so tiresome arise from my longing for "real" life with its promises of exalted satisfactions. My fancies are directed toward life outside, with its temptations, and contrast with the solitary study of my experience. Whenever I conjure up the seductive scenes of lust and delight that await me outside, the atmosphere around me starts to reek of a hospital room.

I am starting to understand the central motive of the displeasure which sometimes accompanies the start of my attempts to delve into myself. I have seen how this displeasure manages to evade my awareness thanks to the shifting nature of the motives, which are constantly splitting up into countless variations which contradict each other ambivalently. I will try to draw up a list here of these many-sided ambivalences.

1. An overvaluation of worldly pleasures, which elevates them to the status of ideals, as if they were the only thing that could give meaning to life. This idealization is necessary to prevent me from experiencing shame at being seduced by exalted sensual pleasures, which would lead to a loss of self-worth and self-esteem.

2. An idealization of myself, which compels me to seek perfection in everything and makes me feel entitled to demand perfection from others so that they may be worthy of me.

3. A devaluation of psychology, since it denies me the right to feel superior to everybody and opposes the excessively seductive image of the world outside.

4. An overvaluation of my secret hope that psychology will disinhibit me sufficiently to open the doors of the idealized world of sensual enjoyment which I crave.

5. A devaluation of myself, since I am incapable of enjoyment, together with an overvaluation of others, who are imagined as being capable of an ideal enjoyment of the world.

6. An overvaluation of the life of ideas, as befits someone whose understanding of and interest in psychology has led him to forsake worldly pleasures and leave their pursuit to vile sensualists, although in truth he is regretfully withdrawing from a world which he is still secretly investing with all kinds of imaginary seductions. . . .

I am aware that I could add endlessly to this list of contradictory combinations of overexcitement and inhibition vis-à-vis either worldly pleasures or the joys of self-knowledge, both of which I simultaneously overrate and underrate. Rather than trying to enumerate them individually, it would be better if I tried to understand the law of ambivalence from which they stem and which governs their disconcerting multiplicity.

Each devaluation flips over into an overvaluation, and each overvaluation corrects itself by means of a devaluation.

This ebb and flow of exacerbated value judgments is nothing but the play of the imagination, continually whetted by wrong motives based on either vanity or guilt, self-pity or accusation. On the other hand, right value judgments, the kind which lead to self-actualization, are outside the fluctuations of exalted imagination and are actually a return to a calm and objective representation of reality, both of worldly pleasures and of the joys of achieving greater insight. In the final analysis, the problem will be solved by giving up the false advantages that vanity provides.

In my progress toward a certain mental balance, I have observed that my escapist fancies and my tendency toward frivolous diversions are far from having been resolved; in fact, they have concealed themselves ever more subtly in order to achieve their fulfillment. Whereas previously my imagination was haunted by visions of unbridled sexuality—this is the most frequent temptation because it is the easiest one to carry out and one most likely to break the monotony of daily life—at this point my greater sophistication has made me understand the need to create a personal bond to accompany the carnal relationship. On this particular battleground, my desire to unleash myself has withdrawn from the engagement, only to resurface in a new shape meant to put me off the track. This is how the search for stability, the idea of marriage, arose in my mind.

Although this idea is in itself quite valuable and its actualization is very desirable, it may also be an attempt to escape the persistent temptation to dissipation. The form in which it haunts me has a perverse aspect, oscillating between the magical hope for a haven of peace and the fear of a shared hell, or at least a ridiculous middle-class existence. The idea of marriage is invested with overwrought promises and complicated with fears, in the same way that my erotic obsessions used to conjure up not real women, with their concrete spiritual demands, but the specters of bodies at the mercy of my whims.

However, even my maddest adventures already concealed the insane hope of one day meeting the young woman of my dreams. Now it is the pure vision of an undefiled young woman—which fate is either reserving for me or withholding from me—which pursues me with its promises of quiet bliss, delightful tenderness, and perfect love. It is only an escape into a new form of unreality: a fairy-tale marriage, as insane as the idea of discovering the intensity of life in sexual indulgence. (I still remember the disgust I would feel whenever, spurred on by my unhealthy curiosity, I found myself in what is vulgarly termed a "wife-swapping party.") All marriages, inasmuch as they involve an exclusive and definitive choice, become illusions under these circumstances. These illusions might very well be the habitual consequences of the vain overemphasis which inhibits any possibility of actually bringing about the thing one longs for.

The point is that when my vanity lusts after marriage instead of debauchery, it is more difficult to detect because it is grafting itself onto a decent, sensible, human aspiration, approved by all—even though I may ambivalently devalue it, considering it moralistic. Given my age, the normal thing would be not to wait too much longer. And yet this very idea of my advancing age associates marriage in my mind with all my feelings of worthlessness and impotence on the material level. The fact that I am forty years old and have not yet accomplished anything makes me feel either unworthy of any woman or afraid that she might push me to strive for material success. Instantly, all hopes of marriage evaporate, and all I can remember is the graveyard of my unfulfilled projects. After my breakup with Geneviève, I have started to be haunted by the idea of marriage. Deprived from a relationship with a woman, on the verge of being obsessed with sexual temptations, I find married life taking on the appearance of a refuge. But might not this shelter turn into life imprisonment? My difficulties with Geneviève make me afraid of a definitive failure, and this anxiety associates in my mind the thought of marriage with the memory of all the setbacks I have experienced in my love affairs, material projects, or business dealings. From this perspective, marriage is just one more "project" doomed to failure. For that matter, this foreboding will actually come true if I do not free myself from the contradictory motives, wavering between excessive hope and anguish, which have always led me into my various undertakings, doomed in advanced to failure.

Thanks to imagination's overemphasis, anguish is communicated from one obsessive project to another: first from eroticism to marriage, then to my social and material situation, and finally to my project of curing myself with the help of psychology—which, being wrongly used, is actually a further attempt at pseudo-spiritual evasion. Imagination's blindness means that the sequence of exalted desires and their transformation into anguish takes place in darkness. Because of this morbid succession, the various agonizing fears I presently feel are not isolated phenomena but the product of my state of mind as a whole, independently of the objects of my fears; understanding this might reduce my intellectual anxiety.

This understanding runs against the imaginary progression and the deceitful tendency to project onto every future undertaking the sum total of my accumulated anxieties. My marriage project is more than just an escape in the face of sexual temptations, which are once more starting to plague me. It is not necessarily an undertaking doomed to failure. Marriage will only become a "prison" if I remain a prisoner of my obsessions. Nevertheless, since the idea of marriage has suddenly become obsessive, it is in part a moralistic refuge which may well lead me to failure. As a rule, the error of overemphasis is concealed in quite innocuous projects, often precisely the ones that appear most morally justified. The wrong motivations contained in these well-meaning projects disguise themselves as pseudo-sublimations, thereby becoming obsessive. The mistake is so subtle and so secret that it would have remained forever hidden to my awareness if I had not been warned of this danger and if morbid anxieties had not forced me to look for a remedy—that is, to review the underlying distorted motives.

« 13 »

The Attempt to Escape

*T*onight, all of a sudden, the prospect of staying at home and sitting down at my desk seemed appallingly dismal. I had been kept overtime at the office by unforeseen circumstances and, after an entire day of work, the idea of devoting myself to psychological study until bedtime was, I felt, more than I could handle.

A woman friend of mine had called me up this morning to invite me out to dinner. I had declined the invitation, intending as usual to spend the evening putting order into my inner deliberations, something which now often gives me a feeling of freedom previously unknown.

On my way home from work, however, my enthusiasm had vanished. The immediate cause for this was undoubtedly my unavowed regret at turning down this morning's invitation, which was still in my mind. Still, to disrupt my mood to such an extent, this regret must necessarily be feeding on more deep-rooted and general causes.

Reality could not possibly seem so unbearably dreary if it were not for the contrast provided by an overexcited imagination. If my interest in elucidation, which has recently been quite sustained, is once more starting to flag, this is no doubt because once again a genuine interest has been overlain by a delusive attraction. In my vanity, I have assigned an excessive value to my work, transforming it into an obsessively important task, a convulsive effort which it would be difficult to keep up in the long run and which must therefore yield sooner or later to the temptation of entertainment. By grafting itself onto my effort, vanity has affected my attraction toward my work, turning it into aversion to an excessive imposition. The pleasure of working has diminished, giving way to dreary automatism. However, even though I have lost my momentum, the vain overemphasis that rivets me to my task is still there. The desire for entertainment which obsesses me is a sign that I am torn between two contradictory temptations which inhibit each other: one denies me the opportunity to amuse myself, and the other makes me regret this denial.

In brief, it seems that I am once again indulging in playing the intellectual, the person of wit and learning, full of dignity. Why not drop this act? Why not reject this game tonight and just go out and have fun? Psychology precludes nothing except overemphasis. Perhaps by reducing my overemphasis on work I might likewise attenuate my overemphasis of entertainment. By bringing both down to the level of natural attractions I might be able to achieve a more objective evaluation.

Whom could I call up? For a while now I have been neglecting my friends, and it hardly seems possible anymore to phone them up out of the blue. What if I called up the friend who phoned me this morning? Would she still be free? But might she not be annoyed with me and reject my invitation, just to get even? In any case, she would think that I am after her. Still, what if I just made a try, without letting myself be inhibited by my suppositions? Picking up the receiver, I dialed her number mechanically. No answer. The idea of phoning Geneviève crossed my mind. Ever since I left her, my isolation has grown considerably worse. We used to go out together two or three times a week—to the theater, to the movies, to see friends. But the prospect of calling her up was not particularly attractive. What do I need from her? At most, I want her body. As for going out together once more and putting up with the constant irritation—never!

I racked my brains thinking of things to do. Should I curl up with a good book? No, I actually feel like getting some exercise. Is it perhaps the call of the street? Night with its magic spell of street lamps and bright neon lights? Crowds released from the workaday world, lusting after easy pleasures? The attraction of sleepless nights, the only way to break the drudgery of daytime? Men and women on the prowl, cruising, driven by the hunting instinct and the illusion of extraordinary adventures? Even while these thoughts were surfacing, I could feel the magic of these seductions rise in me, barely attenuated by the distant memory of previous disappointments.

Why not eat out tonight? As soon as this idea had suggested itself, the image of an elegant restaurant, lively and well lit, came up as in a dream. In this luxurious atmosphere, might I not be looking for something other than the simple pleasure of a meal? The symbolic satisfaction of an unexpressed desire, perhaps?

In the first place, this project seemed like a surrogate for the invitation which I had regrettably turned down this morning. By eating out, I could avoid the loneliness which was weighing heavy on me. But I also needed elegance, the only thing I deem not only worthy of myself, but also capable of compensating me for the exciting evening so thoughtlessly rejected. And is elegance not expressed through women's finery? Already, seated at one of the dinner tables among the other couples, I had discovered the beautiful woman who was waiting for me—elegant, distinguished, sweet, and charming. Seduced by my irresistible appeal, she would come on to me. . . .

In the back of my mind, behind the hazy awareness which was making me smile at such an exploit, a muffled voice whispered in my ear: "You never know what might happen!" So . . . the attraction of the restaurant was in fact a mask for the lure of sexual adventures. No sooner had I focused my awareness on this project than it seemed to lose all its charm. Sitting down in a restaurant in the vague hope of an adventure? Putting myself on display and waiting to be chosen? As a prospect for entertainment, it was rather slim—even ludicrous.

Nevertheless, in spite of this conscious judgment, once the desire for distraction—quite natural in itself although gradually degraded into a desire for debauchery—had entered my mind, it would not stop obsessing me. At last, in order to escape from my musings, I ended up going out onto the street. My idea was to go and see a movie, although I was dimly aware that this was actually a pretext for less avowable projects. So, instead of paying attention to the movies being announced, I roamed the streets for a long time, torn between the wish to turn back and the thought of just drifting haphazardly to see where I would end up. I finally found myself on the Champs-Élysées. Having wandered into this hub of night life in spite of myself, the only thought that came to mind was: "Oh, I'm out of cigarettes. I'll go to a tobacconist's first, and then I'll see what I'll do afterward." As I walked up the street, the thought of abandoning my escape attempt started to take shape. "Isn't my dinner waiting for me? Why not eat at home and then go to the movies?"

This idea had popped into my mind almost against my will—could it perhaps be covering up a trap? Since seeing a movie was only a substitute for my real entertainment project of eating out, I could not really be sure that I would still feel like going out after having eaten at home. If I really wanted to carry out my escape attempt I would probably be better advised to look directly for adventure.

I was probably far from being ready for this, since I suddenly found myself turning back almost automatically and heading home. The suggestion of going out again after dinner was enough to hold my disappointment in check since it surreptitiously left the door open to all kinds of possibilities.

The seduction was still there, but I had managed to blur it enough so that I could drop it temporarily and go back home, albeit reluctantly. In the back of my mind it occurred to me that by continuing to play this game I was running the risk of depriving myself of a natural need for distraction, which had now become unattainable because it had degenerated into a project of debauchery.

In fact, after dinner I no longer did feel like going out. It was too late to go to the theater. Should I walk endlessly up the Champs-Élysées in search of a film to see, hesitating in front of the countless cinemas that line this avenue? If the film has a good review—not always justified—I would have to stand in line, something I cannot stand. Should I just go for any title that catches my eye? I would end up as usual seeing a mediocre film.

I dropped the idea completely. Having freed myself from the pretext of going to the movies, my regret with respect to my underlying project of escape came up in all its nakedness—it could not bear being looked at without a disguise. For a brief moment, I tried to bluff: "Enough hemming and hawing! I'm going out to a café!" I was getting ready to go out, but the spell had been broken. It occurred to me that it might be more fruitful to sit down at my desk and attempt to clarify these no doubt quite morbid alternatives which I had just been torn between. At that point I realized that all evening I had been trying to trick myself into gradually coming to this conclusion. So I ended up staying at home. Here I am, at my desk, not regretting for an instant the restaurant, the film, or the adventure.

The slimness of the interests at stake is certainly remarkable. It proves that nervousness turns the pettiest situations into huge, almost unsurmountable problems. But whatever the real importance of the problem to be solved might be, the inner functioning of my deliberations remains the same. As long as I have not elucidated these contradictory promises of satisfaction—whether distorted, concealed, or, if completely repressed, symbolically disguised—they will continue to control my conscious choices and attempt to define them in a more or less obsessive fashion. Conscious mind, unless it has been completely taken over by this obsessive influence, is in a state of discursive hesitation, often accompanied by hints of actions which may possibly remain unaccomplished. I am aware that the only possible remedy against the assault of subconsciously determining factors is to focus one's conscious awareness on morbid mental functioning as a whole by means of successive elucidations. Guided by previous experience, consciousness will gradually be protected by sane and well-founded evaluations, neither prejudices nor rigid principles, which must be freed from both moralistic inhibitions and trivial laxity. I know it, for I have experienced it.

« 14 »
The Attempt to Understand

To summarize the progression of my thoughts through my hesitations, I think I can safely claim that my behavior on this occasion was not too confused. By preferring to leave the outcome open, I avoided the regret of a forced decision. I was neither disregarding my nervous condition nor blaming myself excessively for it. Instead of being carried away by my imagination, I let my self-actualizing mind take over. Having first of all determined that it is natural to want to have a good time and that anything goes except overexcitement, my reflections maintained a sufficient degree of freedom to allow me to disengage myself from the deceitful attraction of exacerbated escapism and its false promises of satisfaction.

"Anything goes, except overexcitement." I could just as well have said: "Avoid nervous thoughts," since overexcitement is the central symptom of nervousness. At first sight, however, to say that "anything goes" may seem slightly cynical and brutal.

Although their interpretations are often subjective, the existence of moral laws is universally acknowledged. Vague and broad as it might be, the sense of good and evil does exist. Labels have been used to classify it—goodness, purity, generosity, or honesty versus spinelessness, obsequiousness, baseness, or triteness—but that is all that has been done. How, then, is one to know what is good or just, since everyone's opinion is different and since all these opinions contradict each other because they are underpinned by exacerbated emotionalism.

Individuals are responsible for their own lives. They can, in fact, do "anything," but they must accept the consequences; their only alternative is to change their point of view, to impose a free choice upon themselves, a choice which prevents them from doing just "anything." Otherwise, if they refuse to accept this—and that is obviously their privilege—they will be dragged down into suffering by the torments of now overexcited, now anxious and inhibited emotionalism. The notion that "anything goes" is merely theoretical. If satisfaction is important to them, individuals must choose within this "anything" the aspects that are best suited to their intrinsic predispositions. On the one hand, there is responsibility devoid of overexcitement, that is, calmness and objectivity giving rise to different forms of harmony—truth, goodness, beauty, the various "moral qualities." On the other hand, there is overexcitement with its distorted moralism toward these ideals and its retinue of consequences: guilt-ridden anxiety, the temptation to free oneself from it through repression or overindulgence, disharmony, subjectivity, blame, self-pity, the despair of inferiority and superiority, and so on. All these forms of overexcitement lead to irresponsibility, for to escape from guilt one is forced to either deny the value of ideals or to deny each individual fault; both of these alternatives lead to unceasing attempts at deceitful justification. What else can immorality be but the lies that one tells oneself? Can one possibly deny that hidden deep within each human being there exists a veritable arsenal of false justifications, or that these weapons—the armor of vanity designed to ward off the assaults of guilt—have remained absolutely identical from one generation to the next?

The consequences of vain blindness are subject to a law, as are the lucid means of avoiding these harmful consequences. The good that individuals can do to themselves (harmony being the same as agreement with oneself) is measured by one's knowledge of these means, as is the evil that they inflict upon themselves (pathological disharmony). This knowledge, the product of lucid mind, gives rise to the determinants of healthy activity, to motives that are valid on a vital level. In contrast, the constraints of moralism give rise to a purely artificial sense of responsibility based on totally external imposition.

To be effective on a vital level, therapy must involve familiarizing oneself with the arsenal of false justifications and the dangers of their use. By pointing out that individuals are entirely responsible for their fate, it forges the weapon that enables people to take on this responsibility victoriously.

From this viewpoint, therapy is offering me freedom precisely because it does not impose anything on me. "Do as you please, but know that you will not escape from the consequences of what you do. Therefore, it is better to know all the ins and outs of your projects—that is, your motives, the factors that secretly determine your actions. Your psychological sense will be sharpened by your mistakes, and the suffering that will result from them will help you avoid the same trap in the future. This is the way to experiment."

Such is freedom of choice: the freedom to act because one is free to either strive to understand one's motives or ignore them, free to act either sanely or insanely—dragged along by one's overexcitable imagination, "the madwoman at home."[1] Life has an immanent direction which is sane, and which either rewards or punishes. Seen in this essential as opposed to accidental aspect, life's justice is inescapable.

The purity of one's actions depends on achieving inner harmony with oneself rather than on adhering, as conventional morality demands, to externally imposed prohibi-

---

[1]The author has used a well-known classical quote by Malebranche—*la folle du logis*, "the madwoman in [one's] abode"—to refer to the imagination. [Translator's note]

tions. This inner harmony with oneself, the opposite of guilt dissonance, is based on an in-depth familiarity with one's motives—with psychology providing the technique for bringing to light the motives which have been distorted by vanity and escape one's conscious control. Individuals' inability to know their secret motives is strictly commensurate with their dependence on external moral standards, imposed upon them to the extent that they fail to achieve freedom from either trite conventionalism or nervous overexcitement. My receptiveness to both moralism and immorality is a measure of the impurity of the judgments that motivate my actions. Why should I worry about morals that have been forced upon me from outside, which are nothing but moralism?

Only by checking my motives will I be able to discern purity from impurity in my actions and attitudes—this is something I can no longer doubt. Goodness, for instance, is both a motivating feeling and an action; the action is valid only if it is based on the feeling. As an action, goodness cannot be fully realized unless one is capable of detecting the role too often played by vanity—the desire to be noticed. As everybody knows, it is quite possible for an action—say, almsgiving—to be of help to others without being intrinsically valid in itself. The value of an action is inversely proportional to the role played by vanity in its motivation. The force of one's feeling of goodness depends on one's subtlety in perceiving and eradicating vain motives. Our real level of goodness is equal to the ratio of goodness versus vanity; since we cannot be perfect, we must accept this ratio in full harmony with ourselves. Identifying the part played by vanity enables one to detect the real degree of one's goodness as well as gain ever-greater insight into one's relative weakness; it enables one to recognize the distinctive nature both of one's ego (one's means of evolution) and of goodness.

An individual who hears pure goodness, love, and so

forth, being preached may quite possibly overstrain himself in an attempt to achieve the vague ideal that is being presented to him. However, everything that goes beyond his real feeling will only be an obsessive attempt, an egocentric motivation aimed at winning others' esteem and ingratiating himself with them—a form of trivialization, in fact.

However, it is also possible that this trivial suggestion may not succeed in achieving its ends. In this case, the individual feels the deceit involved in his actions; he feels guilty of egotism, and for this he suffers, no matter how imperceptibly. He will struggle against this egotism through actions which, although they appear increasingly generous, involve exaggerated sacrifices which he will be unable to help secretly regretting. The apparent goodness of the act will be underlain by the motive of egotistic regret. As the impetus of both the external act and the internal regret becomes progressively more pronounced, the individual will suffer the torments of nervous superiority and inferiority. He will be caught up in the extreme tension of moralistic goodness, in which the underlying regret may even by entirely concealed by the exacerbation of both the obsessive sacrifice and its vain satisfaction. Who can say that he has never felt, if only obscurely, the reversal of these secret motives, which makes even the most righteous actions come under the suspicion of hypocrisy?

Because of its absurdity, the impulse toward obsessive sacrifice is often repudiated, the regret of continual self-denial prevailing over vain satisfaction. At the extreme limit of this reversal, the individual may deny that goodness has any value, displaying a brutal cynicism whose aim is to smother guilt through an exacerbated justification of egotism.

Understanding the reversals of our motives shows us that it is useless to believe abstractly in goodness or any other virtue, although there does exist a behavior pattern not based on overexcitability, one which gives rise to a feeling of profound satisfaction. The opposite behavior pattern leads only to deceitful surface satisfaction, be it nervous or trivial.

So why should I bother with dogmatism and conventionalism, other than to understand their distorted motives? This is actually my greatest difficulty (as well as the greatest difficulty of any nervous individual): to protect myself from being invaded by wrong motives. Ever since my early childhood, the criteria which informed all the judgments made by people around me were based on sermons about goodness and virtue; these were the daily fare which, in the long run, made of me an egotist incapable of empathizing with others, of sharing their pain or their joy.

Because of this new way of thinking, based on emphasizing inner motives rather than apparent actions and demanding an introspective effort, I am constantly up against the solidly established beliefs of a world that cannot accept being thus contradicted in its way of thinking and acting. Ruffled vanity strikes out in a violent backlash. I am accused of excessive vanity for not believing in the rules of moral conduct set down by "great minds," accused of fixating on a theory which deprives me of any kind of freedom or spontaneity, accused of being monstrously selfish for seeing all actions in terms of my own satisfaction. In others' minds, my referring to motives is just a new dogma; any objections they raise seem perfectly conclusive to them, owning to their prejudice against introspective control. I too adopt the same attitude every time I regard the review of my motives as an imposition from outside. This is precisely why I used the phrase "anything goes, except overexcitement."

I do not mean to say that public opinion should be disregarded, but submitting to others' opinions should not become an obsessive guiding motive.

Others' opinions—the motives of their reactions—have an importance of their own which it is necessary to evaluate and make allowances for in understanding one's own motives. It would be just as vain to fly in the face of public opinion, to rebel against it, as to submit to it. To wantonly defy opinion is to assert oneself like an immature teenager. Thus, I must not go out and tell my friends that their way of looking at life is based to a great extent on a mistake. I would not only make a fool of myself, I would also make enemies needlessly. The reason I am choosing this example is that in the past I have not always kept my mouth shut, and I can still feel the lingering aftertaste of my friends' hostile reactions.

On the other hand, if anything goes except vanity (the principle underlying all forms of overexcitement), why can't I tell my friends what I think as long as I do it without vanity? Surely it is natural to want to share one's ideas with others.

I have just introduced the notion of acting "without vanity," something that is beyond my means. In actual fact, I do not have the degree of self-control that would allow me to calmly interrupt a discussion which leads nowhere. Even if this act were devoid of vanity, if it should happen to expose me to the suspicion of vanity, my vanity would make me seethe with impotent rage. Flustered and annoyed, I would end up feeling guilty for not being able to practice the nonvanity that I preach. My entire vision could quite easily be demolished by the objections which, at that point, I would tend to perceive as unjust and unacceptable criticisms. What this all amounts to is that, faced with my own objections, I take the same position as my friends.

The real issue is not to be without vanity—who could possibly do this?—but to forcefully struggle against vain motives and their false promises of satisfaction in order to reduce their exacerbated—and exacerbating—influence which, when it reaches a certain degree of intensity, becomes the secret cause of a behavior pattern that is obviously morbid. The idea is not to set up new moral standards for myself but to protect myself against the contradictory suggestions, be they moralistic or amoral, which have confused and unbalanced me since my childhood days.

Not having been able to win my friends over to my point of view, the only way to placate them would be to agree with them. Yet I am far too convinced of the truth of my ideas to be willing to reconcile myself with them by sincerely accepting theirs. Nor am I familiar enough with psychology to be able to present my vision to them convincingly. All I can do is either attempt to appease them through courteous though somewhat skeptical approval, or else doggedly try to prove my point, my virulence increasing proportionately to the hopelessness of the endeavor. This would lead to unpleasant polemics in which I could very well get completely carried away by my aggressiveness; the entire situation would then turn to my disadvantage. Humiliated and upset at having lost face, I would give into endless ruminations. Totally demoralized, I would secretly blame myself, others, and psychology. The only result would be that I would have lost my friends. Offended by my excesses, or even by my insults, they would stop seeing me—or else I would avoid seeking them out, ashamed of having made such a fool of myself. Since I actually like my friends and also wish to avoid further and more serious nervous outbreaks, it seems that all I can do is to keep my thoughts to myself.

It is quite sad to be surrounded by people with whom one cannot talk about a subject not only dear to one's heart but also apparently so essential. However, my desire to no longer accept conventional mistakes is stronger than the natural desire to live in harmony with the ideas of my friends.

Faced with this situation, my only choice is to accept my relative aloneness instead of shutting myself off in resentful isolation. Let others live as best suits them. This is the only attitude that will prevent me from getting stuck in morbid feelings of exasperation, bitterness, and sulkiness.

This inner aloneness is a far cry from the anxious isolation of the ivory tower in which I had shut myself off for so long in my nervous shyness and arrogance. Once I have accepted it, this aloneness should not prevent me from discovering areas of possible agreement with my friends—there is always at least one—which will help me to refrain from voicing and spreading ostentatious opinions concerning our differences.

« 15 »
The Dilemma

Should I stop working at Dictio? After all, my incompetence is condemning me more and more to be my partner's workhorse. But whenever I contemplate the possibility of quitting I am assailed by guilt at the thought of dumping everything on Robert's lap. In addition, I would no longer have even this semblance of an activity to help me assert myself before others, at least not in the highly rated field of business.

I have once again fallen prey to the agonizing indecision of a wrong motivation which justifies first one solution and then the next and prevents me from making up my mind. But although the choice I am now faced with is quite serious, I have noticed, much to my relief, that the pangs of indecision have ceased to be unspeakably excruciating and hesitation no longer throws me into a stupor as it used to do at the slightest pretext, even an imaginary one. In dealing with the problem at hand, which had actually been in the back of my mind for a long time, my thoughts no longer degenerate into ruminations. However, I still cling to the disastrous tendency to avoid committing myself either way, to lay the blame alternatively on the situation and on myself and to wallow in vain self-pity. It is this very self-pity which prevents me from observing that, in the final analysis, nothing can force me to work at Dictio other than the imaginary exacerbation of my financial worries and my dependence on others'—and especially Robert's—opinions.

The capital that I had invested in Dictio had saved Robert after he had painfully split up with his previous business partner, who, according to Robert, was preparing to swindle him. However, this investment is all that is specified in our partnership agreement. I am actually free to work or not to work at Dictio; above all, I am free to refuse to be a salesman. The fact that I am the one who can provide cash advances when pressing needs come up is a valuable element in a new business venture whose assets are not large, since we are constantly struggling to balance our cash inflow in terms of our deadlines for paying suppliers. I provide Robert the security of not having to sell off the firm in case of unexpected business losses and enable him to go on adapting to market demands. But to feel compelled to put in actual work—inefficient work, at that—corresponds to no real need.

Nonetheless, in my idea of withdrawing from active involvement I can detect an escape mechanism at work. I was actually aware in advance, at least in general terms, of the difficulties I would have to face, and my purpose was precisely to try to overcome them. It is this failure that is now irritating me. When I went into partnership with Robert, we both knew that we would have to talk to prospective clients. What I did not foresee was that this part of the burden would fall almost exclusively on my shoulders. Instead of leaving, it might actually be better if I attempted to adjust better to office work in order to demand a more equitable distribution of our obligations. Unfortunately, I am so unskilled at office work that I am totally incapable of solving any problem that comes up—quite unwillingly and with no desire to sabotage the firm. My anxieties and scruples have managed to worm their way into my work. The more I try, the more flustered I get. Each problem that arises is transformed into a test. My judgment submits to current opinion and to Robert's encouragement, since he never fails to preach that with a little bit of will power I will be able to tackle the whole thing. But, quite against my will, or rather precisely because of my overstrained will, my inhibitions take over. I am followed by pervasive inhibitions even when I stoop to play the salesman. My entire personality and my entire nature rebel; I cannot help feeling resentful of Robert for supposedly taking advantage of me and even triumphing over me by making me go out and sell our appliances.

The situation is in fact unsurmountable, but only because I can neither stay at Dictio nor leave without losing my calm.

All of a sudden, I find myself remembering my Senegalese soldiers. They were nice, decent fellows. Some of them, longing for an education, would go out and buy the newspaper without even bothering to learn the alphabet. At the end of the day, instead of going out to enjoy themselves, they would put on their glasses and hunker down in the shade of the wall of the drill ground, the most popular spot of all. Unfolding their papers, sometimes even holding them upside-down, they would pretend to be reading. Lips would move in silent articulatory gymnastics and heads would swing from right to left, following each line from one end to the other. Occasionally, one of them would bring his face closer the paper as if to show that his attention had been caught by an exceptionally interesting passage.

This innocent comedy would be of no importance if it were not for its analogical relationship with my own behavior, with which I have probably just established a subconscious association. I have never seen soldiers as industrious as the Senegalese, who were sufficiently educated to attend the classes for corporals in training. What the others were doing was aping the ones who knew how to read; they were behaving just like me, who would like to be a businessman without being ready for it. It was quite something to watch: they would cast sidelong glances all around them to see what impression they were making on each other. The thing that prevented them from acquiring an education was quite obviously not knowing how to read. In my case, the thing that interferes with my work at Dictio is my real incompetence, aggravated by my nervousness. Might it not be better, then, to deal first and foremost with the causes of my nervousness so as to be in a position to make money with a completely different job from the one I am currently forcing upon myself because of my nervous obsession? I can hardly doubt that this is my chance to see where the problem lies, to understand that I am responsible for it and that there exists a tool for reducing it. I must use this tool instead of just feeling helpless in my confusion.

If I leave Dictio, will I have the strength and self-discipline needed to work at my analysis more consistently? Will I have the courage needed to deal directly with the source of my discomfort? The wish to devote myself more intensively to my psychological endeavor is perhaps no more than a pretext for escapism. The fixed scheduled of my work at Dictio may well give my life the framework of discipline I need. Even the irritations to which this job exposes me provide material for reflection, without which the effort at elucidation would often go around in circles. It may be dangerous to reinforce privileges which protect me from excessive exposure to life's struggles, making me yearn for true harmonious satisfaction only during the brief moments when tangible failure has torn the veil of illusion.

If I withdraw from Dictio, will I be strong enough to make full use of the free time thus acquired or will I spend it in entertainment? Will I really have the enthusiasm and perseverance to devote my leisure hours to detecting sudden disastrous variations in my self-esteem?

But if I leave Dictio everybody—my family, my friends, Robert—will take it as a sign of defeatism, of irresoluteness.

Ever since I was a child, I have felt the agony of this accusation. My reaction was either to withdraw in desperation and take refuge in laziness, or else to concentrate all my energies on a task which my anxiety inhibited to the point of making me black out completely, thus driving me back to desperate withdrawal. Could there possibly be an analogy between my childhood behavior and my desire to withdraw from Dictio in order to focus on the therapeutic process?

This is quite possible or even plausible; in fact, this is most certainly the case. But the aim of keeping a diary is precisely to free myself from my infantilism. The effort of writing it demands not only mental receptiveness, but also the use of my leisure time, which I should normally be able to devote to relaxing. In addition, ideas do not come to me only when I sit down at my desk, open my notebook, and start writing. They constantly come up, throughout the day. They take over my mind, as if they led a life of their own at my expense. They unfold in accordance with their own analogical links. They mate—if one can use this expression—and give birth to analogical consequences. Whether I like it or not, they are present within me and demand to be rethought, assimilated, and formulated. My resistance to psychology may come, at least in part, from this influence, which I feel corresponds nonetheless to the best of myself. Since I am inclined to clarify my reflections, to care for them, to nourish them with my time and energy in order to derive the greatest possible benefit from them, I find myself forced to interrupt them prematurely, going so far as to lose all traces of their development. These are the moments when my work at Dictio becomes a real torment, a handicap which seems insane and which, when all is said and done, I accept only because of my dependence on the opinions of my partners, friends, and relations—my fear of public opinion, to put it in more general terms.

At this point, I am toying with the idea of neither rebelling against social demands nor bowing to scornful accusations, but simply accepting them. Let people think whatever they will—if I choose to act this way, it is for my own good and I am not hurting anyone. Unfortunately, this is easier said than done. Nonetheless, although it is quite unpleasant to be misjudged, it is even more painful, more unhealthy, to go reluctantly against one's own judgment in order to be better judged by others. Of the two evils, I will choose the lesser.

After forty years of the obsessive fear of not being valued by others, of longing passionately to be pampered, accepted, admired, and understood, it will be quite difficult for me to accept people's favorable or unfavorable opinions calmly and simply go my own way without worrying about them.

The infantile yearning to be understood has pursued me all my life! To free myself from this infantilism is the prerequisite for being cured. This childish desire has already lost a great deal of its exacerbation, and I have noticed that it decreases proportionately to the insight I acquire into myself. By understanding myself and my condition in life, I can achieve freedom from the obsessive fear of being misunderstood or of not being looked up to by others.

Hopefully, I will succeed in distinguishing more clearly my inner motives and the data of my social situation since, on the one hand, they compel me to exercise a profession and, on the other, they make me struggle to free myself from it.

I feel that leaving my work at Dictio puts me in a critical situation since my inability in business will prevent me from finding another job more suited to me. It is not impossible that this step will speed along my cure, yet I wonder if it may not lead me even deeper into bewilderment. The fact is that by living without a defined profession I will be exposing myself not only to the disapproval of my family and friends, but also to generalized ostracism.

From a social point of view, one's livelihood is one's most characteristic trait: "And what do you do?" "Oh, I have a degree in this or that and I practice such-and-such a profession." People's curiosity has been satisfied; they know what to expect. One has been classified according to one's value in social competition, according to one's skills.

Until now, I have been able to answer this question. I have avoided acknowledging that I am in fact no more than an ordinary sales representative, taking pleasure in referring to my status as co-owner of the Dictio firm. I have showed myself in the most favorable light and avoided the unfavorable judgment to which aristocrats, supposedly enervated by their privileges and unable to face the hardships of this day and age, are exposed.

The benefit that I derive from being one of the bosses of the company is actually very mediocre. However, my anxiety at the prospect of losing this reassuring advantage may well be one of the reasons for my indecision. What answer will I be able to give indiscreet questioners? I would be wise not to indulge in thinking that I am sufficiently emancipated from public opinion to be able to fly in the face of its most entrenched judgment.

Until I am able to come up with an undeniably valid judgment of my own to oppose to this conventional judgment—if only deep within myself, without even needing to exteriorize it—I will always be haunted by the feeling that not practicing a profession discredits me in everyone's eyes, exposes me to the accusation of being a parasite. This is probably why I am tortured by indecision every time I try to think about the issue. The fact that everybody has a trade ensures the existence of a material basis for society. It seems selfish to withdraw within myself, to turn my attention to my inner woes instead of integrating myself in society and submitting to its inescapable demands.

This is the central problem that all political discussions deal with. What does my enthusiasm for psychology mean in the face of the ebullient fanaticism with which people defend their stands on social issues? If their justifications are all spurious—this is precisely what I would like to believe—

who can assure me that my own reflections aimed at legitimating my withdrawal from my profession are not also false justifications?

Yet, if I were to give up my job in order to enter the monastic life—if I were to shut myself up in a cell instead of in a room—not only would people not object to my abandoning collective duties, but they would almost unanimously respect me. Public opinion is in favor of religion. This is undoubtedly the crux of the matter. But why should I not be entitled to choose and to prefer psychology? If my intention was to spend my time collecting stamps, I might not be held in very high esteem by others, but at least I would not feel like a social outcast. No matter how pitiful this project might be, it can at least be pigeonholed and understood by public opinion. But what about the detailed study of motivations?

What I aspire to is to stop taking part in the production of material goods. However, the issue never fails to acquire vast proportions. Rather than limiting the problem to Dictio, a business concern of rather paltry significance in terms of "public welfare," I tend to ponder the appropriateness of my decision in relation to current ideas on spiritual life and society's material demands—no matter how absurd all this may seem to me. I put myself in the position of my supposed opponents and experience in my mind the assault of their opinions and judgments.

I should no doubt consider the issue in a totally different light. What is the use of generalizing my tiny problem? My excessively emotional criticism of the social question is only an attempt to conceal my fear of being criticized and accused by society. This exacerbated demand, directed alternatively against public opinion and myself, is probably based on the nervous individual's well-known tendency to be satisfied only with absolutely perfect solutions.

This pattern is undeniably present in me, as it surely is in all nervous persons. It explains the tendency to always demand the impossible perfect solution, which makes every solution that is put forth subject to criticism. This pattern of demanding absolute perfection also explains the second tendency, ambivalently opposed to the first: to dogmatize one of the solutions offered, elevating it to the status of absolute truth in the hope of avoiding the agony of bewilderment. The truth is that this agony of bewilderment is probably the root of all forms of nervousness, including my own. The demand for absolute perfection is perhaps only the exacerbated antipode of the too real inadequacy of so many of the solutions that are advanced. Who knows? Perhaps the most characteristic trait of the nervous individual is precisely this need for a superstructure made up of true ideas and guiding ideals, with the disastrous tendency to demand perfection being no more than a caricature of this. How does one build this superstructure?

No matter how often I try to let go of my tendency to understand things thoroughly, I cannot bring myself to do it. And I have certainly not created this problem for myself in an arbitrary manner. This seems to be precisely the dilemma which my dream pointed out to me when it presented me with the choice of the pen of greater insight versus the dress suit of appearances. It might be better, then, if I stopped dwelling on the social question. Yet the need to achieve a more thorough understanding would surely lose all its meaning if I backed out of any problem that arose, and especially if I avoided the social question, the most debated issue, the one most overlain with emotions and therefore the most thorny one.

This may actually be our "thorn in the flesh." Embedded in our minds, it irritates us to the point of making us suffer in the flesh since it exacerbates material desires—not to mention "carnal" desires—and poisons all human relationships, not only between individuals, but also between social classes and nations.

I certainly do not wish to find a solution to the social

question, bogged down with contradictory ideas as it is, but only to find a valid outcome for my own social situation. It is precisely my stubborn dependency on these contradictory ideas that gives rise to the indecisiveness of my old apathy.

If only I could be like so many other people, smarter or more sensible than I, who commit themselves to a single idea or guiding ideology, whether right or wrong; in this way they manage to find their bearings in life and are able to act as well as can be expected.

My mind reels. . . .

After so many attempts to clarify my thoughts, one thing seems to me more unquestionable than ever: the individual and society are inextricably intertwined. This is why it is necessary to untangle them through analysis, which is exactly what I have attempted to do in order to get a clearer idea of the limits and demands of social life. I have not succeeded; this is probably because my ability to see clearly is still too weak or because I have gotten completely carried away with vague generalizations.

If I feel unable to come to a decision with regard to my "professional" problem as it presents itself in my personal social situation, should I not submit the question to the analyst instead of exhausting myself in vain attempts to figure things out, attempts which leave me more perplexed than ever? Should I not acknowledge that my project of detailed daily self-analysis through these journals conceals a pitfall for my vanity, and that it might become far more dangerous if I decided to devote all my time to it? If I am not careful, these journals will lead me to try to resolve the problems that arise from my mental confusion single-handedly, without having the necessary tools, instead of submitting them to the analyst so that he can help me find a way out—if this way out exists.

The decision to place myself in the analyst's hands is probably the only valid idea that emerges in the end from this evening's fruitless efforts.

« 16 »
My Cousin

I have just left a distant cousin with whom I was very close during my childhood. It was really a great pleasure to see him again. Our meeting brought back happy childhood memories of those long-forgotten days. Then we came back to the present. I told him that people never spoke about him without praising his intelligence and his brilliant career: the École Polytechnique,[1] a happy marriage, beautiful children and, at forty years of age, already a "big shot" in a very prestigious company. Yet in spite of everything, he remains a gentle, nice, unassuming person.

Why did I mention Dictio to him? It was, I suppose, the most natural thing in the world to do, since we were talking about our lives in a spirit of friendship and mutual appreciation; but as soon as I referred to my project of leaving work in order to devote myself entirely to psychology, the charm was broken. I was no longer on the same level as he: he had gotten up on his horse, and quite rightly. He looked right into my soul and saw the fear of life that grips me like a vise, the lack of courage that makes me run away from practical matters and take refuge in abstractions.

In leaving Dictio, I am actually fleeing from concrete things. As a matter of fact, I now remember that the idea of quitting started to take shape one day when I was explaining

[1]France's most celebrated school of engineering and one of the *grandes écoles*, or "great schools." [Translator's note]

to Robert the misgivings I felt concerning our company's future. However, in my cousin's opinion, the future of the appliances which we manufacture is very bright. In fact, he considers them so essential that he intends to outfit his own company with them, and therefore asked me to give him a demonstration.

Not for anything in the world would I have accepted to supply him with our product, for in spite of the positive results of the tests, I have my doubts about how well they work. In my eyes, selling them has always involved an element of conmanship. The idea of leaving Dictio might in fact also be motivated by my desire to wash my hands once and for all of the dishonesty required to ensure our firm's survival, to no longer wait for Robert—who, quite free from any feelings of guilt, takes excessive advantage of the situation—to develop for our customers' sake a more satisfactory product that can be mass-produced. By not withdrawing my investment, I could return at that point and get a share of the profits. These are probably my true secret feelings, even though they may be disguised as an infatuation for psychology. In fact, why pretend that I would not be interested in a company that had at last become honestly lucrative?

Be that as it may, I felt obliged to confess to my cousin why I did not want to play the dirty joke on him of supplying him with our product. I explained to him that the company that Robert and I ran was actually minuscule. He was extremely surprised that we had been able to manufacture such a complicated machine under such conditions, even though its operation was not quite up to scratch: "You need major capital investments, engineers, consultants." I agreed with him entirely, realizing that I had been more or less aware of this for a long time but had refused to acknowledge it, preferring to wait for the miracle to happen. Not wanting to give the impression of living in a world of illusion, I decided to draw his attention to my leaving Dictio. "Can one stay in a firm that's doomed to failure?"

Unfortunately, carried away by my boastfulness, I found myself forced to explain what I would do upon leaving and started to talk about psychology. I remember quite distinctly asking myself at that point: "Is the reason you're leaving Dictio because it's not lucrative or because you're interested in psychology?"

As soon as I mentioned the word *psychology* my cousin picked it up with enthusiasm: "It's really fascinating, psychology. All major corporations and industrial concerns hire psychologists, as you probably know. There's a real need for psychological consultant firms with sections specializing in various industries, all of which are urgently crying out for psychological expertise. If I just had the time, if only I wasn't caught up in the system, I would much rather turn my attention to the human soul instead of dealing with machines, steel bars, aluminum bars, turnovers, and balance sheets. To put the right man at the right place! But also to adapt the object to people's tastes and needs and thus achieve common satisfaction!"

I timidly tried to interrupt his flood of words to tell him that this was not what "my" psychology was about. However, I did not dare to confess that I was mainly interested in self-analysis and that I would be devoting all my time to acquiring true knowledge about myself; to spend all day gazing at one's navel, that would be sheer madness! I told him that I had put my trust in a doctrine, a vision of life, based on research by Freud, Adler, and Jung, and I took pleasure in laying great stress on my involvement with a group devoted to studying the thought of Paul Diel, its leader. He actually listened to me at first, more attentively than I would have expected. So I let myself get a bit too carried away and spoke to him of the dawn of a new age, heralded by a psychology that had at last become a science, complete with its laws and its experimentation. I fear that my excitement made me reckless and I went too far. My cousin admitted that this project must be quite exciting and did not fail to tell me how much he envied me for being able to take a leave of absence and devote myself entirely to it. Had he been independently wealthy himself and able to lead a comfortable existence with his family, he too would no doubt have dropped everything: his profession, his business, his worries, and the heavy responsibilities which never stopped hounding him. "You don't know how lucky you are!"

Then he asked me for further details about my studies: "What degree will you get when you graduate?" None, I answered, since this study goes against all the officially accepted and recognized theories. "Do you write? Do you intend to publish? Do you people give lectures? Then what is it that you do, in practical terms? What exactly is your involvement in all this? Unless I've misunderstood you, this Diel character has just invented a new theory—maybe even a very extraordinary one, who knows? That's wonderful! He's presenting his ideas, and you people are reading them and discussing them—fascinating! I myself remember how much I enjoyed my philosophy classes." For, while studying to become an engineer, he had also gotten a general arts degree and even won a prize in a contest. Warming up to the topic, he added: "It's an intellectual game which makes the mind unbelievably keen. All these theoretical systems are more or less intelligent speculations. They're not the truth—that would be too much to ask. Besides, their partial falsity causes new doctrines to blossom. They're all facets, detached aspects of an ungraspable whole. It's fine for the inventor of a new theory to get all excited over it. It's all right for him to devote his entire life to it. He has discovered something, so he presents it, publishes, and makes a name for himself. He corresponds to a moment in the history of ideas and influences his period of history—for better or for worse, by the way. But you and your friends, surely you must know that all doctrines are relative! It's normal for a professor to study them in depth, since they're part of his curriculum. It's fine for you to do it out of intellectual curiosity; knowing the various theories that have been put forth gives you a broader view of the world, one more complex and sophisticated. It's also quite natural for one particular theory to influence you more than the others—this gives your general knowledge a more personal stamp. Great! But all of this is not a valid end in itself. Intellectual games demand tolerance. If everybody became a passionate and exclusive disciple as you seem to have done, nobody would have any food on the table and all the famished disciples of the various other schools would have no choice but to devour each other. . . . "

He then explained to me that life is first and foremost practical and that playing around with abstract ideas may help one acquire greater culture, but should not make one lose sight of reality. Far from being an aim in itself, the study of ideas is only a means to sharpen action. Activity thus becomes more subtle, turning away from the pursuit of mere material profit and personal interests, away from one's trifling complaints, one's petty egotism, one's intrigues, becoming finally more generous, more human, part of a greater vision of the world. "You know," he told me, "the work I do for my company would kill me if it only involved manufacturing. My real interest lies in the ongoing research that helps the corporation meet everyone's requirements, from the workers right up to the bosses. The idea is to continually improve the organization, so that everyone can fulfill his aspirations. Obviously this cannot be done in one day. But if we, who happen to be more enlightened because of our material privileges, which give us access to culture—if instead of cutting ourselves off from the world through vain intellectual masturbation we decide to leave our selfishness behind and come down to the level of practical everyday life, we might actually be able to influence our entire age, leading it toward greater justice and welfare. If we're brave enough, we might even be able to tackle injustice head-on, to denounce it, and, in accordance with our greater or lesser capabilities, to gradually create a current of common activity which would slowly gain momentum. Only such active involvement can free mankind from exhausting labor. Give everybody material goods and leisure and, through leisure and universal education, they will then have access to culture. In brief, everybody should be given the same material and spiritual privileges. You might say that some people are just beasts of burden, incapable of any kind of reflection. Yes, I do know some factory workers who refuse to make the minimum effort needed to become skilled workers. Still, although they may only know how to stick the nozzle of an oil can into a machine that needs oiling—a machine they can't be bothered to learn anything about even though they know that by working on this machine a few hours every day they can bring home the bacon—at least if they're paid better they'll enjoy a decent standard of living and be able to go fishing on Sundays if they feel like it!

"Of course, we're nowhere near this yet. But since automation this has become a plausible scenario for the future. And it's a future which people like you and me, endowed with a greater and more generous vision, can bring about as long as we are not content to merely envisage it and shut ourselves off in our thoughts, but are willing to help prepare it through concrete activity. And I'm not just talking about the manufacturing field: all of the other industries can take part in this progression toward a superior order. You used to paint, didn't you? Well, then, you should know that painting's more than just merrily spreading colors on a canvas in the hope of getting rich; it's allowing people to share in the beauty, it's giving them access to a more uplifted and refined taste, to higher aspirations, so that they can aim for ever greater culture. Before painting you were in the military, right? God knows if there's anything more stupid than boot camp. But to get in touch with your fellow men, to talk to them, to take interest in them, their families, their problems, their hopes, to be able to give them advice, to help them individually—that's a real task! Do you remember X? Recently he told me that many of the men who had been under his orders still drop in occasionally to see him, to talk about themselves, confide in him, ask his advice or opinion on a matter, or simply chat for a while, just for the sake of being with another person, out of gratitude for having met a friendly soul in a world where human beings are few and far between and will remain scarce if everyone who is capable of establishing such contacts defects and withdraws from the world of men. . . . To sail away into the subtle and rarefied atmosphere of ethereal, disembodied abstractions, where mind tickles itself like Gargantua trying to make himself laugh—that's a cop-out, a form of cowardice toward life. You know that as well as I do."

I am swept along by his arguments as if by an avalanche. Yes, I am aware that my cowardice, my avoidance of the world, life, and people, my ineptitude, and my lack of courage are so strong that I am only able to enjoy solitary pleasures in which I am alone with myself: skiing, because I am lost in the crowds rushing down the slopes and because I can fall without hurting anyone else; riding, because horses are docile; reading, because life's adventure is disembodied in fiction; Dielian psychology, because I only have to deal with myself. I really do not care about my internal mess— after all, I am used to it, I am the first to find myself cowardly, stupid, sordid! I am more willing to contemplate my shit and my uselessness than to expose them in action and lay them open to others' distaste and ridicule. Psychology takes on the appearance of a wonderful haven where I can avoid humiliations, including the ones I am subjected to at Dictio. In comparison with these situations, being humiliated before Diel, before a single person, is nothing at all. It is also quite flattering to feel supported by someone who is willing to take an interest in you. It is entertaining to talk and to have others talk about oneself, to become the center of the world, to devote oneself exclusively to observing, dissecting, and analyzing oneself—to playing with oneself, in other words. A perverted pleasure, when you get down to it. What wonderful slothfulness, what a splendid pretense of activity to stay comfortably at home and study "psychology" while others, including Robert, struggle and exert themselves, facing life's difficulties and overcoming the resistance of time, space, objects, and people.

How did I ever disengage myself from this discussion which had demolished me completely, showing me that all the things that drive me toward psychology are only false pretexts?

I no longer even know whether I am coming or going. Somebody just comes along, and here I am, bewildered and gasping for breath. I feel stuck, fixated on that discussion, or rather on my cousin's monologue, having been totally incapable of coming up with any kind of objection. Toward the end, I was not even listening properly, trying instead to think of the objections that Diel himself might have made—I still am, but to no avail. Of course, I could ask Diel himself. However, since I will not be able to play the part of my cousin and defend his arguments as he did, Diel will change my mind for me completely, just as my cousin did. I feel like a pancake, which any skillful cook can flip over on one side or the other according to his whim. Even when I am exposed to heat on one side, I do not acquire a real consistency. It is the frying pan that is rigid; I remain soft, molding myself to the contours of the pan, capable only of taking on the shape of whatever mold I am poured into. I am like a mollusk, no matter what shell I slip into to try and give myself the illusion of having a definite form of my own. Perhaps the smartest thing to do is to take psychology as my shell, once and for all. With my soft hermit crab's ass

stuffed snugly into a theory, I could contemplate the world
with all its fuss and bother—but would that be living? Will
I even have the courage to tell Diel that for me psychology
is no more than a shell now? But if, for fear of losing his support, I do not tell him, my project of devoting more of my
time to it would take on a fearsome aspect. What can I do,
then, if all of life is charged with dread? I am fed up with
this life in which everything eventually turns against me,
since I have no solid opinions on anything. A magazine arti-
cle is enough to get me all excited and win me over to the
author's point of view. But if I attempt to communicate my
conviction by remembering the arguments that convinced
me, they vanish at the first objection, and I am surprised that
I did not myself think of these objections, which made me
change my mind completely. One would think that after
years of reading, listening, and discussing, I would have
grown distrustful of my own gullibility. Far from it—every
time, I just remain flabbergasted, dumbfounded, and panic-
stricken, observing my own defeat. Inevitably, I end up
feeling humiliated, ashamed, desperate. I can expect nothing of myself.

Me, a psychologist? My cleaning lady has a much
sharper mind than I! She never lets herself be taken in by
anyone, and her judgments of the people whom she deals
with are always quite accurate. My cousin, who only met
Robert once over dinner, immediately noticed how talkative he was and guessed that he must be a charming but not
very serious person. And in me he immediately perceived
the morbidity which drives me to look for theories which I
can take for cash. And yet, and yet. . . . Might I not be falling prey to my most morbid fault: to turn my vain
justifications into excessive self-blame?

Rereading my notes, I find myself staring at the page,
haunted by a nagging feeling of discomfort. I have the definite impression that I have made a mistake, that I have
indulged in a tearful mockery. What is this if not a form of

vanity? And who opened my eyes and helped me learn to make out the existence of these vanities in their countless disguises and transformations, although I may have just fallen prey to them?

My reaction to my cousin's attack was to stupidly transform into excessive self-blame the vain self-justifications that underlie my idea of leaving Dictio, in itself quite justified. This is the reason for which the apathetic nervous type is constantly changing his mind. The image of the pancake being flipped over takes this fault to the unbearable and misleading extreme of self-accusation. Because of its very overemphasis, the exaggerated confession of the fault turns into repression and vain pseudo-objectivity. Once again, I am faced with the two ambivalent poles of all forms of overexcitement. How many times has Diel warned me about this, adding that only introspection will convince me that this is so? Here I am experiencing that conviction—will I let myself be intimidated by the image which I have chosen and set up against myself? Intimidated to the extent of not daring to hope that there will be a new change of mind, a healthy one this time? I have suddenly understood, with all the clarity I could ever wish for, that what I have just blamed myself for so vehemently is not to have let myself be influenced by Diel, but to have let myself be dissuaded by my cousin. How can I possibly have been so blind that I did not immediately see that all of his arguments were drawn from the arsenal of sophistries of one of the most fashionable false ideological justifications? Driven by a desire for revenge and one-upmanship, I could just as easily have turned the disparaging image against him and compared his viewpoint, which he stated with so much pseudo-conviction, to a pancake which has molded itself so well to the frying pan of conventionalism that it can no longer be unstuck. Whether I use this image against myself or against my cousin, it has both an element of truth and an element of falsity. It is in the nature of our images to be valid only to a certain extent, and then to inevitably become false when they are taken for explanatory realities.

So I had better drop this excessively disparaging image, whether I turn it against myself or against him. This will allow me to come back to reality and to review the excessive conclusions which I have drawn from this image, without fearing that I will be once again subjected to a perverted reversal.

My cousin is perhaps a better psychologist than I. But better than Diel? If, as he claims, ideas are good only for theoretical games, why does he put forth his own ideas with such conviction, as if they were the ultimate truth? It is a mediocre psychologist who does not notice that all his pettifoggery only amounts to a big production meant to convince himself and to persuade me that he has a mission in life. It is a perfect example of false justification. The mission of the managerial elite? Any factory worker would be able to reply to him with extremely justified grievances; if the worker has the slightest imagination, he will have no difficulty in finding arguments to prove that it is actually up to the working class to carry out this mission of justice, which would involve getting rid of the missionary boss.

If my cousin were a poor employer-employee like me, who am actually neither employer nor employee, he would perhaps stop preaching the virtues of the managerial elite. His imagination, more fertile than mine, would find the justifications which I look for in vain in order to free myself without scruple from a situation which is, after all, quite absurd, my work at Dictio having become unbearable. The absurdity that has led me to this situation has also helped me come up with a splendid excuse, since I have absurdly started thinking that in order to cure myself from my absurdities, I need only devote myself to the mission of being a psychologist. Does Diel, who contends that he can cure me, claim to have a mission too? Are we all absurd beings who like to think of ourselves as missionaries?

Is life per se absurd, a senseless piece of nonsense? If so, what should one do? Anything at all? Even something senseless? Even the most senseless thing? Kill time any old way? Unleash depraved appetites, which by being unleashed would become more depraved? I would find this more deadening than exhilarating. Can one possibly become attached to senselessness? I have seen people destroy themselves through drugs, alcohol, sexual adventures that soon turn sordid. . . . They are lucky to be able to get high on this—I soon found the whole thing quite sad and sickening.

So what now? Should I blow my brains out? That would be the escapism to end all escapism, the height of absurdity, the supreme temptation of apathy!

No. Life must have a meaning, a sane direction, values to be discovered. Senselessness in itself is the void in which all values are lost—as are all nonvalues, absurdity having elevated them to the status of values. If everything is senseless, no thought, no action would have more value than any other. There would be no value, no hierarchy of values. To live or to commit suicide would have the same senseless nonvalue. Whether I kill myself or whether I murder another, mind in its senselessness would be unable to distinguish better from worse. At most, it would be able to provide me with spurious justifications which I would take for valid motives. It would be no more absurd and no more just for a mother to kill her child or to raise it. Even the satisfaction which she might derive from either of these actions would not be a criterion for value. Would she kill her child if her imagination led her to believe that this would be more satisfying?

As for me, one certainty guides me: the problem of existence is called life and death. I find it more satisfying to live than to die. Whether it is senseless or not, absurd or not, there is nothing that I can do about it. I have until the end of time to be bored in death. As long as I live, I will defend myself against boredom. And the best defense is to reflect on the essential problem of greater or lesser sanity, greater or lesser ethics, greater or lesser health. It is this reflection that I would like to devote the rest of my life to, even if to find the path that leads beyond mind's erring ways I may have to deepen my knowledge in the most unexpected ways.

« 17 »

The Dialogue with the Analyst

I spoke to the analyst about my present problems. Having taken care to record on tape the session devoted exclusively to his reply, I am transcribing it here in its entirety. Diel agreed to edit the text in view of eliminating needless repetition and adding further explanations. In inserting these pages into my diary, I thought it might be useful to break up the text into three parts.

I

Diel: The pages of your diary you gave me recently bear witness to the extent of your present state of hesitation. But the troubles you were suffering from when you first came to see me can be characterized in terms of your dissatisfaction over social situations and your inability to make a level-headed decision which would solve the problem. Your apathy did not exclude sudden pseudo-decisions— poorly thought out, wrongly motivated, short-circuited, if I may say so. Instead of liberating you, they plunged you into feelings of failure and ruminations of regret, signs that you had relapsed into apathetic indecisiveness.

So I wonder whether your hesitation with regard to your project of leaving Dictio on the pretext of concentrating on your study of psychology might not be preparing the ground for yet another short-circuit reaction.

Myself: But surely you must be aware that thanks to

your help I am no longer quite the same person I used to be. Can't it be possible that this time the decision I have to make is so important that my hesitations are justified?

D: You may be right, I agree. However, if you really intend to devote your time to an occupation which you find more interesting, why not work part-time? That would allow you to see if you are actually able to concentrate on your project, without burning any bridges.

M: Of course! Why didn't I think of it before? How can I possibly be so blind as to lose all sense of moderation, all good sense? And I thought I was sufficiently aware of my nervous pattern of going from one extreme to the other.

D: Mind you, I find it quite understandable for you to be toying with the idea of throwing off your professional responsibilities, if you can call them that. It might be better to put an end to these pseudo-obligations, the vestige of a previous state of mind that is not very compatible with your present focus of interest. In the first place, the material privileges you enjoy mean that your project is not unreasonable. But it would be good for you to earn these privileges; otherwise, they could turn against the nervous individual that you used to be and that you still are, to some extent. They could turn into guilty anxiety. This is the reason you tried to submit yourself to the social demands of practicing a profession. Yet material privileges do not necessarily corrupt; money can also be a liberating force. Take the saying "Time is money," a trite slogan inviting people to kill time—their lifetime—in the pursuit of money. Taken to its extreme, it leads to venality. But one could just as easily turn the expression around and say, "Money is time": money actually frees time. It all depends on how you use the time thus freed. If it were just a matter of switching professions, the problem would be quite simple. All you'd have to do would be to weigh the usefulness of each. Essentially, nothing would have changed. You'd continue to participate in the production of material goods—which is necessary to ensure comfort and certainly nothing to be sneezed at. But you would like to acquire free time by no longer participating in the excessive overproduction which transforms desirable conveniences into the inconvenience of compulsive work.

Don't force yourself to be part of a ruthless struggle for subsistence. But don't forget that freeing time for yourself only makes sense if you also set your mind free. What would you do with the free time you'd acquire if your mind were still a prisoner of all the slogans and prejudices hammered into you since your childhood and upheld by extremely powerful ideologies for which the meaning of life lies in the overproduction of pseudo-conveniences? Your hesitations derive from the fact that your mind has not sufficiently liberated itself from the overconsumption of erroneous ideas and your personality has not quite emancipated itself from the greediness of desires. The uneasiness you feel, the fact that your mind is bogged down in ambivalent scruples, comes from your dread of succumbing to these desires. The most trivial justifications would suffice to overrule all your scruples if all you wanted was a changeover from being an idle worker at Dictio to being an idle student of mind. But actually, what you're contemplating is the prospect of devoting yourself to studying the complex workings of mind, a project that would lead you away from every possible lucrative or reasonable social situation. To do this one needs force of conviction upheld by extraordinary interest, by interest that goes beyond the ordinary. Only time will tell if you're capable of such conviction—that is, supposing that you do commit yourself to this path. For me, your apprehensiveness about the outcome of this project is by no means a conclusive proof of real inability. It is just as likely that your interest could be roused and that, reasserting itself, it would triumph over inhibiting anxiety. Perhaps your state of indecisiveness is due to a doubt you feel deep within yourself, with regard not only to yourself and your abilities, but also the efficiency of the method you're intending to devote your time to. Don't repress your doubts—face them! If you're interested in deepening the knowledge you've acquired about mind, but nevertheless inhibited by the prospect of a decisive commitment because you're afraid of being on the wrong track, there's still another way to participate in the study of mind: why don't you consider the possibility of studying general psychology, its history and its various doctrines?

M: I'm not really all that interested in studying general psychology. My abilities and inclinations go only as far as acquiring a deeper understanding of my own existential problems.

D: But your most obvious existential problem is finding out what it is you're committing yourself to! By studying the history of psychology, you'd come across every conceivable objection to the method of self-observation.

M: I've never really seriously doubted the method. Besides, why would I want to object to it anyway? It's given me an incredible sense of relief.

D: That proves nothing about the objective validity of the method. Don't you know that the most diverse methods can pride themselves on achieving good results?

M: What does prove a method's validity?

D: The only way I could answer that would be by first helping you face your doubts and then confronting them with what I have found to be true.

M: That's exactly what I was expecting when I asked you to read my notebook.

D: You seem to want me to give you an overview of your entire analysis, with its foundations and objectives, which would get us away from your present practical problem of making a concrete decision. We can certainly come back to this attempt to deepen our understanding, enriched, I would hope, by new elements that might allow you to focus clearly on the motives for your project and to respond with a decisive yes or no.

M: That's the purpose of my question.

D: Well, what we need then is an unquestionable statement.

M: Is there such a thing?

D: Sure, and it's quite simple: only the quest for truth, whether it concerns mind or the world, is beneficial.

M: That's pretty obvious.

D: Well, then, would you like us to take this obvious statement and together try to find the countless unsuspected motives for your indecision with regard to a problem which apparently couldn't be more simple? I have never suggested we do anything but look together. As you well know, the whole difficulty comes from the fact that in the depths of our mind and its functioning, there exists a spurious possibility of liberation, a wrong path of inner deliberations in the form of obsessive and unhealthy beliefs. What is indisputable is the fact that in our daily life, our reasoning is often troubled by emotions. Affective thinking leads us to illogical conclusions and subjective convictions, phenomena so widespread as to be rarely included under the heading of "mental illnesses," although they're quite likely a first stage of mental illness which most often passes unnoticed. Don't we sometimes obsessively believe in intuitively perceived ideas which we elevate to the status of truths?

M: Absolutely—it happens all the time!

D: And it's a phenomenon of the greatest significance! In fact, truth and error, far from being merely abstract phenomena, become motives for action. The source of insanity is hidden where one would be the least inclined to look for it—in our own mind, whose sole function is supposedly the quest for truth. It's not the natural fallibility of our mind, the fact that it's prone to make mistakes, that's to blame. On the contrary, this possibility determines the function of reasoning and the search for the reasonable, which are specific to human beings. The entire process of rehabilitating mind involves detecting the error and confronting it with truth.

Morbidity involves sabotaging this process through emotional blindness, which instead of correcting the error, tries to pass it off as truth. Mental illness is the temptation to wrongly justify one's errors, which results in wrong motivations for one's actions. Would you deny the existence of this temptation to create false self-justifications?

M: On the contrary! Even the slightest introspective act is enough to convince me of this.

D: On the other hand, everyone perceives more or less accurately the wrong motivations and false justifications of others.

M: Analysis has made me aware of the unsuspected degree to which I indulge in this. It's shown me how rejecting truth jeopardizes one's mental clarity, how it degrades it into daydreams, which are the first stage of subconscious obsession. Repressed doubts condense subconsciously into doubts about ourselves, disagreement with ourselves, guilt feelings. This continual repression of doubt removes guilty anxiety from conscious control until it finally bursts forth from the depths of our subconscious as irrational and symbolically disguised psychopathic symptoms. This is at least what I think I've understood. But I don't see how it ties in with my present problem.

D: We'll find out. On the level of inner deliberations, all problems, whether material or sexual, depend firstly and ultimately on mind's right or wrong assessments. Since the purpose of inner deliberation is to elaborate voluntary decisions, all instances of indecision are the consequence of one's mind being more or less blinded by vanity. We are all producers and victims of our false self-justifications, even when we don't end up in the extravagance of hallucinosis. Nothing can be more beneficial than to stop disregarding this truth, which we can observe through introspection. It should be accepted as the methodical basis of all research, whatever the field, for the value of any form of research depends on mind's lucidity. But since mind is a psychological function, it is mainly psychology which, by admitting the primordial truth of the existence of false justifications, will go from one discovery to the next, each one more beneficial than the previous one. Stated in this way, the problem is knowing how mind can free itself from its own unhealthy temptation.

M: I am starting to see all the secret doubts I harbor about your method. On the level of ambivalence, psychology has become a blind faith, a lifeline I cling to in my distress. But can mind possibly have the power to free itself from its own tendency to vainly justify its mistakes, from its oscillation between exacerbated belief and sterile doubt?

D: Indisputably, since its real purpose is knowledge rather than belief or doubt. The exact sciences are there to prove it, especially physics, which has set the standards for other sciences with its rationality. It studies the rising and falling of bodies, the laws that govern their movement. There's no emotionalism to trouble the serenity of research. Affectivity is not upset by the laws that govern the rising and falling of bodies. Mind's satisfaction, the joy of knowledge, leads here to technical applications, marvels of ingenuity which, in just a few centuries, have transformed all the conditions of our existence.

Psychology, on the other hand, should study the laws that govern the rising and falling of the "soul." In the same way as physics studies external motion, psychology could study internal motion—emotions and motives—which are too often the cause of illogical and irrational behavior. It is tremendously sad to realize that, because of this tendency to fallacious justification, the mind of any given human being can be in the process of falling while imagining itself to be actually rising, and that the fall can be all the more dangerous if vanity is making the mind think it's rising. This makes the problem of vanity or the temptation toward false justifications—illogicality par excellence—central to our study. By studying this distorting principle and its innumerable justificatory disguises and by formulating a method of lucidly approaching the study of our inner logical or illogical functioning, we can make psychology into the "science of life," paving the way for technical applications which we can hardly imagine at this point. At the very least, we can provide for its modest beginnings. However, for want of such a science, the inescapable need for a sane orientation remains unsatisfied. The problems of practical living create a situation quite different from that of the exact sciences. In highly specialized research, no bonus is given to the deviations of vanity. Only scientists—those who know—are entitled to speak, and all researchers are united by a common method.

On the other hand, as far as the problems of living are concerned, everyone attempts to put forth his own solutions, usually haphazardly gleaned conglomerates of unchecked intuitions and doubtful opinions. This results in a situation which is quite intolerable. There is only one truth, and this truth leads to oneness; this is its life-giving force. Mistakes are manifold and contradictory, and result in a veritable orgy of well-intentioned improvement schemes, heterogeneous insights, and ideological biases, all armed with an arsenal of false justifications.

M: Obviously. But it seems to me that not everyone can have the same opinions. . . .

D: But it would be good if everyone was at least aware of the insanity of this state of things.

M: One can object that truth has many facets.

D: No part of the truth can be in contradiction with any other. One should be able to bring together all the facets into a harmonious whole. This is the very definition of science and of its search for laws.

M: I know I would be wrong to suppose that you're imagining a world where everyone would be an expert psychologist.

D: In the same way as a physicist would not demand that everyone know the details of his science. A fairly limited number of researchers is enough for the whole world to be able to profit from science's technical applications—if the world is able to do this reasonably. But even the misuse of science can't be used as an argument against its progress. Why should it be otherwise with curative psychology? Unfortunately, it is far more difficult to achieve tolerance in this field than in others. What I would like to establish at this point is one of the most basic aspects of life-giving truth: the distinction between true and false tolerance. Note that the term *tolerance* brings together the two highest qualities of the mind: lucidity and warmth. If, out of self-indulgent pseudo-generosity, you insist on being tolerant toward the quarrel of opinions, which generate resentments —and the tone of your voice reveals to me your underlying irritation—you will necessarily remain at least partially intolerant with regard to the only really beneficial truth. This truth stipulates that freedom of mind is falsely defined by everyone's right to present his or her opinions as truth. Freedom can only be acquired through self-discipline, through the effort to liberate mind from its perversion: the false justification of opinions that are all too often wrong. As long as this morbid state lasts, it's important to be tolerant, in view of the present lack of a science of life. Does that make you smile? You're perfectly right. I'm not so naive that I don't know that this definition of tolerance might seem too demanding.

M: To a lot of people it might seem like the height of intolerance.

D: As long as they mistake indulgence for tolerance. And what if this mistake were only a special case of the false justification which confuses just and unjust, true and false, and false and true? It would seem to me that the height of false justification would be to demand indulgent pseudo-tolerance with regard to the weaknesses of the human soul, yet to be intolerant with regard to the inescapable necessity of mobilizing mind's immanent force, its love of truth—in this case the truth about mind's own healthiness or unhealthiness, the truth about ourselves. Does this endeavor seem too subjective? Don't worry; its aim is objectiveness with regard to self and other. Incompatible with intolerant or pseudo-tolerant resentments, self-objectivization, as you yourself have probably realized since we started working together, happens gradually through daily introspective experience aimed at eliminating resentments.

M: Which are the only various manifestations of vain self-justification?

D: Exactly. Objectivizing tolerance, while being a subjective quality, refers to interpersonal relations. Its other name is humor with respect to the ambiguous nature of everyone's minds, torn between truthfulness and justificatory lies. Humor is being able to laugh at ourselves, at our common weaknesses—a tolerant laugh, qualified by the confidence in our common strengths. Everyone has good and bad points. What varies from one individual to another is not only the specific pattern, but also the particular intensity of each. Objective tolerance is the ability to understand, with the necessary degree of humor, that life in society, all social situations and institutions, all currently accepted ideas and prevailing ideologies, are the sum total—a quasi-mathematical product, if you wish—of the truths that have been discovered and the errors that have been mistakenly justified.

Wrongly motivating justification creates injustice in each person, and activity spreads it out over the world. Tolerant humor, in its widest sense, understands that on the essential level of inner deliberations we all make exactly the same mistake: we wrongly justify our erroneous ideas, thus resulting in wrong motivations for our actions. In this tolerant vision, humor realizes that our common suffering is the punishment for our main fault—a fault which is found entirely within ourselves. It is not that we are partly to blame and the world is partly to blame, for the fault is based on distorted deliberations; therefore, everyone is entirely responsible for it. The habitual misunderstanding of this indivisible responsibility destroys tolerant humor since it unfailingly makes one lay the blame excessively on others while exonerating oneself completely. This mutual resentful blaming becomes the secret cause for our common suffering, since it makes everyone suspicious of everybody else, extending suspicion ultimately to the world and to life. Everyone partakes of the repressed inner cause of common suffering in accordance with the degree of intensity of his or her own mistake: the wrong interpretation of oneself and of the world. This illness of mind manifests either as nervousness or trivialization. Immanent justice could not exist without a law to enforce punishment of mistakes. This is the tragic humor immanent to life. Mind becomes tolerant by adopting this humor as its own, by understanding the deepest cause of the human tragedy. But mind can't do this without introspective self-criticism which, seen from this angle, is actually humor, since it is trying to overcome the tragic—otherwise tolerance would only be pseudo-generosity. Extended to all of life and concentrated in a guiding vision, this tolerance/humor draws its strength from the hope—the conviction, even—that mind will be able to overcome its own weakness, however long this evolution may take. Haphazard insights and good intentions will not suffice to lay the ground for the revolution of mind. Nothing but the unbearable increase of morbid suffering can wake mind out of its stupor, imbuing it once again with combative spirit. The illness itself becomes a vehicle of good, which is the love of truth and the joy of knowledge. But this combative spirit, mind's highest quality, can only be mobilized deep within each individual, where it is often blocked and deflected by the influence of prevailing ideologies. The ultimate definition of true tolerance is its combativity, its ethical courage. Combative tolerance attacks not people but wrong ideas with their false justifications.

M: If false justification exists, then everything is distorted. Everything is other than what we imagine it to be.

D: Obviously. And this would imply that everything must be changed—everything we think and everything we do.

M: I find your conclusion slightly puzzling; it seems to have gone too far. Still, at least I understand the foundations of your method a lot better. As a whole, they seem justifiable. . . .

D: Unless they result from wrong justification.

M: I didn't say that!

D: But one has to say it! If false justification were the only psychological reality, everything would be open to suspicion. But if—as I never fail to stress—self-critical thought exists too and can be used as a method, then everything becomes clear and open to change.

II

M: But what if objectivizing self-observation is not possible?

D: That's what some people claim. But is there anyone who could deny that, before acting, he doesn't deliberate with greater or lesser lucidity? And what is this deliberation but constant introspection aimed at assigning values to our desires and sorting them out according to their promise of satisfaction, thus preparing the motives for future actions? The factor that is capable of valuing, the opposite of the blind grasping of our sexual and material desires, is called "mind." Self-critical mind is often flooded by the blind affectivity of desires; this is such a frequent phenomenon that it can legitimately be labeled "trivialization." Linguistic usage has always resorted to terms like "mediocre," "ordinary," or "run of the mill" to designate it. Can one possibly imagine that deliberating mind's only function is to falsely justify its potential debasement into triviality and that self-critical deliberation is only a delusion? Don't forget that according to the wisdom contained in language, the aim of inner deliberation is liberation. What should it liberate us from if not trivial baseness? What can take on the truth-seeking function of inner deliberation other than mind itself by becoming aware of its danger of enslavement? No, objectivizing self-observation is not impossible. Granted, making the individual psyche wholesome again is difficult, but that is all the more reason to develop it into a method.

M: But society and its institutions may not be designed to make individuals' deliberations any wiser. . . .

D: True; however, that's only a partial and inadequate truth. Traditions, even when they have become institutions, are themselves no more than the product of individual leaders whose deliberations were more or less sane; they also happen to be controlled by individuals whose motivations are more or less sound. The issue of inner deliberation is primordial. For the individual, psychologically speaking, social institutions amount to promises of satisfaction and threats of punishment. In this way they elicit individual adjustment. Like all environmental solicitations, they are the subject matter of our inner deliberations. However, it is individual deliberation that determines individual adjustment or maladjustment; from it springs the voluntary decision on which social intercourse depends. Our reactivity to the solicitations of the environment is first and foremost a product of the mind—the term *mind* referring mainly to the deliberating function. Behavior, the habitual action patterns which characterize an individual and make up his specific personality, is also a social phenomenon, but only secondarily, as a consequence of "interreactions." These interreactions are underlain by each person's right or wrong motivations, developed by a mind that assigns more or less sound values. As long as the individual tendency to false justification lasts, there will always be social injustice. What this means is that adjusting to flagrant injustice does not make people any saner; this can be achieved only through the individual struggle against vain self-justification, which tends to evolve into self-idealization and self-glorification. Excessive self-glorification implies excessive indictment of others, of the world, of life. All social relationships are thus overlain with aggressive resentments, the hidden motives for never-ending and deceitful mutual provocation. This is the real issue of social life. The equitable distribution of material commodities is only one of its many aspects. Every human being likes to think that he or she is the only blameless person on earth, while being seen by everybody else as part of a guilty environment. The tragic part is that everyone's complaint—the consequence of forgetting his or her own participation in collective injustice—always contains a justifiable core: others as a whole do actually participate in everyone's conspiration against everyone else, since we are all producers of wrong justifications and therefore unjust actions.

Note that these observations reinforce the notion of combative tolerance as the only real remedy, both for societies and for individuals. This is because individuals' social actions are codetermined by theological, philosophical, and even pseudo-scientific ideologies which societies pass down from one generation to the next through socialization so that their members don't have to begin the process of deliberation from scratch and so that everyone is deliberately available to practice a profession and participate in the production of material goods, considered as the most important social function.

No : . . . helping people to adjust exclusively to the material demands and prevailing ideologies of any given society is not the same as healing them; all this achieves is to turn confused nervous individuals into trivial go-getters.

The error lies in confusing sociability with social life. Sociability is a psychological quality, an inner feeling which extends to all human beings no matter what society they belong to. Social life, on the other hand, is the arena in which resentments confront each other. Admittedly, one of the purposes of psychotherapy is to help the individual adjust to social reality, for nothing would be more erroneous than to neglect the analysis of social relationships. But true adjustment means to give back to the sick mind its own lucidity with regard to the ideological errors which keep it from understanding society or the individual.

M: I suppose that if I were to study psychology, it would be just as wrong—just another false justification—to examine inner deliberations exclusively as to focus solely on social influences in their more harmful forms . . .

D: Or in their more beneficial forms! For, quite obviously, beneficial social influences also exist. The reason I'm stressing introspection so much is that it's been put down so often. But since one's environment does nourish and feed one's deliberations continually, it would certainly be necessary to contemplate it in much greater detail than we have just done.

Its study requires a complementary method or, rather, ancillary techniques: external observation, in its statistical and clinical forms. As you know, statistics allows one to compare an individual's capacities with the average for the population of his milieu, whereas clinical observation is essential in curative psychology. Methodical introspection reveals the laws that govern mental formation and deformation; clinical observation reveals the multiplicity of psychopathic symptoms and is the basis for their classification. In addition, clinical questioning is necessary to identify the patient's past and present social environment. Obviously, when a curative intervention involves the use of drugs exclusively, understanding the inner workings of the patient's mind may seem quite unimportant. But the moment the therapist ventures to give advice, this poses the problem of psychology in all its seriousness.

Many people possess a psychological knack, based only on habitual introspection though devoid of any method, which helps them give others more or less sound advice. However, even in the best of cases, the disappearance of a symptom is not a sign of a true cure, for this can only be achieved by making the deliberating mind wholesome again. Neglecting to use introspection as a method, clinical observers are content with more or less haphazard results. Conversely, some curative methods have been developed from unavowed introspection; they will perforce remain contradictory, because they are combined with speculative elements.

M: Nowhere can half-truths be so harmful. . . .

D: Undoubtedly. But one should not forget that depth psychology, pioneered by Freud, was broadened by Adler, Jung, and many others. In their works one can find many passages that stress the importance of introspection. Precisely because we're dealing with depth analysis, achieving a deeper understanding is essential. Having established this as a method, the unfolding of truth goes beyond the limits of research inasmuch as each new development opens up new horizons. This leads me to an observation which will be my conclusion.

There is one decisive fact that makes me insist that the importance of the social situation, however great, is never paramount. Not only are we always, without even realizing it, being self-critical observers, which determines the guilt feelings we all too often repress; but our constant deliberating introspection exists also under another, much more captivating, fascinating, and alluring form, which shows us much more tangibly how unbelievably easy it is to let oneself be blinded. Psychological reality, the universe of deliberation, is not a microcosm, as we might like to think;

it is just as vast and enormous as the macrocosm. We carry the entire universe within us in the form of images.

M: I don't understand what you mean.

D: The spectacle of life is presented to us through sense perceptions. We call it "reality." But the world as perceived externally corresponds, feature for feature, to a world imagined internally. As soon as the perceptive watchfulness demanded by presence of mind is lost, an imagined "re-presentation" starts to unfold within us, which encourages and even results in absent-mindedness. It pursues us through our night dreams and manifests even more frequently as wide-eyed daydreams. We are the spectators of this internal spectacle; this is what "introspection" refers to. The thing is to direct one's awareness to this inner spectacle so as to subject it to self-control; for we are more often deliberating under the spell of this spectacle than in terms of perceived reality which does not allow us the leisure of musing over things but forces us to act immediately. The internal spectacle is not static but dynamic. It represents not only external objects, the goals of our desires and the causes of our fears, but also recalls past situations and foresees situations to come. We are the heroes who act in this internal spectacle, and this can enable us to observe ourselves critically as long as we don't fall into either vain self-admiration or excessively self-deprecating inhibition.

As long as we remain critical spectators, this imagery will be a more or less objective representation. Promises of satisfaction and threats of dissatisfaction are embodied in images which file past our inner-directed gaze. The action motives which are thus formed correspond pretty well to real possibilities. But there's a great temptation to detach critical mind from this imagery and to direct it affectively toward the external world in which our desires are constantly being thwarted by the exacerbation of others' desires. When internal imagination tries to console itself by escaping from the reality of both the thinking ego and its environment, deliberation becomes morbid. The exacerbating power of escapist fancies is unlimited; its omnipotence is capable of satisfying in advance, through pure illusion, any desire, whether pseudo-spiritual, material, or sexual. Devoid of self-criticism, distorted spirituality becomes an accomplice of this evasion and attempts to justify it. The contrast between imagination and reality—the source of suffering—becomes more serious and may even become pathogenic. Reality is finally imagined to be hostile and unjust, no longer only in specific situations, but in principle, because of its very existence. Cut off by this excessive exacerbation from any real possibility of satisfaction, desires progressively become degraded and turn into inhibiting anxieties. Hope turns into despair, and imagined omnipotence flips over into real impotence, whether sexual, material, or spiritual.

Even though in psychological terms they may be a reality, escapist fancies are insanely unreal. Vain justification makes this situation worse by adding illogicality; having repressed the mistake which creates guilt, loss of contact with one's ambient reality leads to loss of truth with regard to oneself. Mind becomes unwholesome, gradually losing its capacity for self-control, its power of sound deliberation. It can no longer grasp either reality or truth. Feelings[1] are degraded into resentments, which destroy any human warmth, whereas will is dissipated in vague impulses,[2] which are alternately exacerbated or inhibited, thus determining behavioral deficiencies.

M: This describes not only my previous state but also my propensity to morbid introspection.

D: It also describes the liberating technique. Faced with the seductive force of exacerbating imagination, good

---

[1]The French words for "feeling" (*sentiment*) and "resentment" (*ressentiment*) are related etymologically. [Translator's note]

[2]The French words for "will" (*volonté*) and for "vague impulse" (*velléité*) are related etymologically. [Translator's note]

intentions are helpless. As long as one has not reviewed one's motives lucidly, their false promises of satisfaction will deliberately produce wrong reactions. Liberation can only be achieved by ridding one's inner deliberations of their wrong calculations of satisfaction of which motives are the elements. Since blindness arising from escapist and justificatory fantasies operates at the threshold at which imagination surfaces into consciousness, its ill effects are subject to self-control.

The liberating technique which I've set forth deals with the internal spectacle. Rather than remaining an indulgent spectator one must mobilize one's self-critical thought and its objectivizing force day after day. Easy to say, but not always easy to do—that's why, as far as the curative method is concerned, it's essential that one deepen one's understanding in both analytical and synthetic terms. Based on analytical self-observation, this deepening synthesizes past experiences into a general assessment of the good and evil that we do to ourselves through either wholesome or unwholesome deliberation. As an immediate outcome of the analytical experience, synthesis gives rise to theory with no need for speculative intervention; theory in turn becomes the guide for wholesome activity by suggesting sound value judgments that will prompt one to avoid evil, ill-being, unwholesome situations, and mental illness.[3] Only by deepening one's insight can one see the relationship between false promises of satisfaction— false because they have been radically exaggerated beyond any possibility of fulfillment—and their pathological and inhibiting consequences. Rather than remaining guilt-ridden, through perseverance self-criticism can gradually acquire foresight and lucidity and take on the challenge of relinquishing the exhausting pursuit of unfulfillable projects and accepting the conditions of ambient reality as

[3]All these words are etymologically related in French: *mal, malaise, malsain, maladie psychique*. [Translator's note]

unchangeable. This releases energy, which can then be used for the fulfillment of sensible desires.

When you were experiencing this in the course of introspection, you would always attempt to place yourself lucidly in relation to your world and social environment. On the other hand, you would often forget to do it in the midst of any given real situation if you gave into escapist fancies, false justifications, or vain scapegoating, accusation, and self-pity.

M: Yes, that's what analysis has showed me. I will try to practice this more and more all the time.

III

D: So let's draw a conclusion from your experience and your in-depth study of your experience in order to help you overcome your present conflict with respect to your decision. You have acquired a method and a technique which will ultimately allow you to go on improving your condition without the help of a therapist. What is there to prevent you from pursuing this health-giving experience without devoting all of your time to the study of its theoretical underpinnings, which could expose you to the risk of a new and more serious relapse into vanity?

M: So you advise me against it?

D: I'm neither for nor against it; all I'm doing is suggesting that you examine your motives. That risk does exist, but it is not unavoidable. If this overview of deliberation and its objective of liberating the mind and the personality has managed to assuage your doubts and reduce your hesitations, I'd be quite willing to admit that your project is not a vain pretension but corresponds to a real need. The truth of life and its meaning is a scarce commodity with which the market is inadequately supplied in both qualitative and quantitative terms. Why not then try to produce it by yourself and for yourself, unpretentiously, without trying to haggle over the time of your life? You're smiling? I wasn't joking. All the things we have been trying to understand together can be condensed into a single formula, which is far from being a slogan: internal success is more important than external success. Think about this until it soaks into you. This precise formulation brings about a radical change in our wrong approach to our projects and problems. It summarizes the entire process of acquiring deeper insight.

M: It also contains the answer to all my questions.

D: One could come up with further objections. One could go on inventing objections forever.

M: May I summarize them all in a single question? It kept going through my mind as I was listening to you.

D: Don't repress it.

M: What if the whole world were to say you're wrong?

D: How would that make any difference in terms of the existence of inner deliberations, of false and true justifications, of the entire gamut of mental activities—the only things that can make us feel pain or pleasure, that can make us live and act?

M: That's true.

D: The technique I'm giving you to help you lead a happier life and suffer less is subject to improvement. How could it be otherwise, since this is true for everything we do? But this process of improvement can only be based on deepening the introspective experience. Don't be afraid of objections. They'll only touch you if you secretly carry them within you. No doubt you'll be criticized for your solitary retreat. And if people think that it's an escape from life's difficulties, I can assure you that the most effective way to tackle all of life's difficulties is to reflect on their secret inner causes. It's true, however, that such a life involves one major disadvantage: it narrows the field of your experience. Enlarge it, if you wish, by establishing the cell that recreates society: the family. You must realize that all too often the troubles experienced by societies come from the fact that couples get bogged down in resentments, which they then transmit to their children, and so on from one generation to another. In exposing yourself to the most difficult experience of all, an experience much more difficult than your professional life, you must fight the resentments that arise, day by day. Transform them into warmth, for only through warmth will your relative solitude become wholesome and bearable. If you wish, go on writing down your difficulties in your diary if it helps you find valid solutions. But most of all, don't ask yourself whether your writings show talent; what counts is whether they're effective in terms of building your character and improving your life. But I'm getting carried away giving advice. . . . Whatever you decide, I hope it does not plunge you once more into the indecision of regret.

M: I'm so glad that my recent indecisiveness sparked off this summary of your method and its raison d'être. I was already familiar with several aspects, but I'd never heard it synthesized and articulated so clearly. To really assimilate it though, I'd need to listen to the tape once more; I'm really happy that I'll be able to listen to it over and over again.

D: That's the best way of achieving soundness and precision of judgment.

M: Thank you.

D: One more thing . . . Oh, no, nothing! There'd be too much to say; the topic is inexhaustible. We'll have many opportunities to reflect on this together again. And also by ourselves.

« 18 »

The Decision

Robert has the obnoxious habit of engaging me in a conversation just as I am about to leave the office. As I was leaving for lunch, he started telling me about the sale problems which would arise once the business expanded.

"You're right," I told him. "A good salesman is really hard to come by. Any company that has something to sell is always on the lookout for good salesmen. It requires a certain skill, a gift . . . luckily it's not a matter of intelligence, because that would mean I'm quite dumb. But maybe I am dumb after all since I can't really help you run Dictio. I'm totally at sea. I have difficulty keeping up with what's happening, and I don't dare make a move for fear of botching things, as I always seem to. Besides doing a few demonstrations, which any employee could do better, I just hang round the office, bored to death. Basically, what I'd like is to cut down on my hours at the office and come in only part-time. I'm working on an interesting project at home right now, something I've just gotten into. If an emergency comes up, you know where to reach me."

"I can't keep you from doing what you want, so you may as well go ahead. However, I have a hunch that we're going to expand pretty soon, so there'll be plenty of interesting projects for you right here."

"At this point, I'm quite bored with the whole thing. I'm talking about myself, of course. As far as you're concerned, the situation is quite different. You were the one who started this business, and your management responsibilities make it interesting for you in spite of all the difficulties. Can you picture yourself as an employee in a large corporation?"

"No, obviously not. But I'm sure that you're not as incompetent as you think. Still, do as you think is best. Just remember that soon, when the new model is ready, it'll be necessary to supervise production, deal with suppliers, start advertising again. . . ."

"I could actually manage all that. But until that point, as long as I'm only involved with selling, I'd rather just come in in the mornings instead of hanging out all day."

I had been afraid that I would meet with endless objections, but actually everything went very smoothly. It did take a bit of persuading, but by sticking to my point I managed to get what I wanted with no loss of cordiality. We parted quite amicably.

How deceitful and formidable the imagination can be! Not long ago, it would have taken me over completely, filling me with dread and inhibitions. This attitude could in fact have triggered the objections I was afraid of. I would have submitted unwillingly to them, seething with rage at my impotence, which had once again been proven to me. I would have either turned my rage against Robert or curtly demanded my freedom, leading inevitably to a stormy separation. But I was simple, natural, and firm and did not lose my presence of mind, because I knew exactly what I wanted. I was convinced that my cause was justified. I was not ashamed to defend it, and there was no rebelliousness in my action.

However, I shouldn't make a big deal out of this calmness. Vanity is lying in wait for me, and bragging would only lead me to cruel disillusionment. In fact, the power struggle with Robert is not over; my putting order into my motives has merely made it retreat into the background. This proves nonetheless that by identifying vanity and be-

coming aware of its vain promises and morbid consequences, one can actually make it regress and decrease in
intensity.

The countless aspects of psychological prediction can
be condensed into a single observation: when vain desire is
repressed instead of being avowed, it turns into guilt anxiety
and sterile remorse. This relationship between false promises and actual ill effects usually escapes conscious control.
The mistake lies in thinking that I must become perfect and
throw off the influence of vanity completely.

Although there will always be vanity in me, as in every
human being, one can reduce its intensity. Vanity must be
made to lose its seductiveness and remain in the background
to prevent it from condensing into an extravagant task,
which, by becoming the center of all one's morbid preoccupations, gives rise to excessively obstructing character
deformations or even obsessive symptoms. For someone
who, like me, has all too often gone astray in emotional
blindness and exacerbated imagination, keeping vanity in
the background demands constant watchfulness.

My compulsive desire for perfection prevents me from
being content with improvement and makes me believe that
I can free myself from vanity in one fell swoop. This is why
I would like my therapist to give me a clean bill of health
once and for all, since this would make my effort at self-
control no longer necessary.

I remember having this feeling as a schoolboy working
hard to get my diploma—or rather daydreaming about getting it, absurdly thinking that by succeeding I would be
forever free from all restrictive demands. But as my horizons broadened, the effort which my parents' arbitrariness
had apparently imposed upon me was succeeded by life's demands. My immaturity makes me see problems in a childish
way. As long as I remain in this frame of mind, as long as I
remain lethargic and infantile, I will continue to rebel
against the prospect of life imposing upon me the effort of

elucidation, which I will be unable to see as anything but a burden.

The truth is that I must replace fallacious deliberation with a lucid review, which will save the time and energy I all too often waste on fanciful ruminations. What I need is to make my deliberations wholesome. This sudden insight puts everything that Diel told me in a nutshell.

The effort to achieve a more wholesome form of deliberation is actually the only thing that can give life its intensity and its deepest meaning, which is the right against secret self-deception—no matter how subtle, whether morbid or not, even if conventional wisdom advises one to ignore it. As long as this arrogance lasts, as long as it refuses to yield and goes on turning my life into an arena for pretensions, I will be inclined to pursue my self-analysis in the sole hope of someday (if not right away) achieving an Edenic existence and living happily ever after in a state of perfect innocence.

This spurious promise of a future Eden, this vain hope of one day resting in a static perfection which would free me from the dynamic effort of improving myself, secretly contains the tangled roots of all my false motives. Unless I am constantly watchful and aware of this inordinate hope, it will always be ready to change once again into guilty anxiety and will never cease to infiltrate the motivations for my behavior—including my present attitude toward Robert, which is temporarily more just. False feelings of triumph would arise once again, becoming a real threat for our relationship before long.

In my car, having left Robert with a feeling of relief after surviving the ordeal, something was already starting to give way. I had a vague sense of discomfort, a feeling of discontent made up of self-pity colored with guilt toward the friend I was abandoning. But a ready-made justification had already suggested itself: "I'm not cut out for such a vulgar job." One more step, and the accusation took shape: "He at least is made for this pathetic trade."

I had pulled it off. Robert had become for me a synonym of Material Labor, and I was suddenly the Representative of Psychology, the Defender of Mind. Seeing material contingencies as radically opposed to mind, I was once again shut off in the ivory tower which rises well above the contingencies of material life by Psychology, the symbol of mind. Yet the very loftiness of this superb isolation was cause for alarm. Even as I was savoring my "victory," I was suddenly panic-stricken, overcome by vertigo at the huge self-imposed psychological task which awaited me. The time which I had meant to put aside for this project seemed to me like a gaping vacuum into which I would be plunged and lost forever, with no hope of ever getting out.

My conversation with Diel has put my thoughts into a state of effervescence. Ideas swirl madly though my mind, trying to crystallize. All the better. However, I must attempt to regroup them into a whole through my own reflections.

Advance turns into retreat and desire into dread—these imaginary somersaults make me long for what I cannot have and look down on what is within my reach, be they spiritual or material endeavors, entertainment or concentration.

In this state of mind, I seek comfort in the image of the psychologist which I sometimes profess to be. Exacerbated hope oscillates continually from the spiritual to the material and then back to the spiritual. Even though my inability to achieve self-esteem at Dictio leads me to believe that I can get it from psychology, I pay for this vanity with the agonizing feeling of being no more competent in psychology than in any other activity. This transformation of exacerbated desires into anguish is perhaps one of the expressions of the justice inherent in life.

To attempt to satisfy exclusively spiritual demands might be just as much of a mutilation as the exclusive search for material satisfactions. Mind and matter being inseparable and complementary forms of life, each takes on a monstrous aspect if the other is excluded. If adjustment is to be wholesome, one should not ignore these two ineluctable and complementary demands. Only very pure and very rare minds—saints or wise men—are capable of remaining in the lofty heights of spiritual life without the air becoming too rarefied for them. If I have understood Diel correctly, this is not the aim of the psychologist, who aims rather at achieving harmony between mind and matter. Since this concord, this satisfying harmony, is continually upset and must be constantly reestablished, it remains a constant object of study and self-control. Never being in a static equilibrium, harmony must always be dynamically re-created.

My error lies no doubt in the fact that I am continually turning this problem of mind versus matter over and over in my mind with my theoretical reasoning, playing with both directions and opposing them so radically that I feel impelled to look for a perfect solution. Why not be content with finding a relative solution, like physics when it calculates the resultant of two forces brought to bear on the same point?

Since the attempt to elucidate is motivated by my dissatisfactions, it continually leads me into excessive abstractions and makes me forget the concrete link between mind and matter. The reason for this seems to be the fact that I am prey to an image which I mistakenly take to be reality and which incites me to oppose mind and matter as if I were weighing them on a pair of scales. This imagination, which makes the most fundamental relationship of life a mechanical one, might in fact be the origin of my defective viewpoint. Balancing mind and matter against each other, I am led to materialize mind excessively, for in order to outweigh matter, mind must necessarily be falsely endowed with a weight of the same order. When I think of "matter,"

I see trees, the earth, women, money, a house, a car, the sky, the clouds, the apparent world and myself as a soma, the central character of this apparent world. On the other hand, I assign to the word "mind" a value which I would like to be just as palpable, just as visible, as if mind were the most beautiful object among all the objects I would like to appropriate. But mind could not be the object of covetousness if it were not for my vanity, which tends to materialize everything, even mind, in order to turn the fact of owning it into a credential.

All the liberating value of apparently theoretical psychological reasoning resides in the fact that it compels us to discover at last the error of vanity which lies hidden under every ideological development as long as this development, influenced by false images, opposes the only reality: the dynamic unity of mind and matter, of self and the world. The blindness born of excessively static images, this blindness of the imagination, disturbs the cohesiveness of ideas. That is why even in the realm of ideas, it is important to review vain motives in order to unmask the error.

In our culture, mind[1] and matter are too radically separated. Mind tends to become excessively moralistic and material desires excessively seductive. I must continually rediscover this disruptive error within myself until such a time as my vision, the guiding principle of my activity, is sufficiently liberated. The word "mind" is all too often empty of any real meaning. Mind is not an entity that hovers above material life. The term "mind" is no more than a linguistic sign that designates a psychological function: the need for elucidation, a factual phenomenon which I experience in many ways, even in its negative forms of doubt or guilt clinging stubbornly to the mistake. Emotional blindness and its lack of objectivity come from excessive attachment either to mind or to the external world. What

[1]The word *esprit* in French means both "mind" and "spirit." [Translator's note]

could be the meaning of aspiration, the active experience of mind, without the reference point of external reality and the possibility to achieve mastery over its temptations? What every person longs for, often quite unconsciously, is surely to organize his or her material and sexual desires in view of achieving inner harmony, the source of joy. This yearning for oneness in one's character and coherence in one's ideas seems to be the basic impetus which drives human beings, manifesting through truthful mind with its power to consciously dominate matter and material desires, both at the individual and the collective level.

Mind is not a theoretical entity; it is not something absolute that exists outside of matter, independently of my body and its desires, which attach me to the world around me. It is a relationship and exists only in relation to matter. It is the true relationship between the world and the self, both on a theoretical and on a practical level. Well-informed psychologists are no doubt familiar with this relative nature of mind. But for me, a prisoner of current prejudices, the vision of this relativity and the modesty it implies are a discovery of capital importance. This discovery will help me to the extent that I am able to make it into a living and life-giving idea, a guiding vision which can heal me from my radical overemphasis on mind—the mental illness par excellence since it creates its own counterpole of exacerbated attachment to the earth. In fact, these ambivalent poles are the basis of my suffering.

This reasoning, apparently too theoretical, reveals to me quite clearly the practical mistake which I had made earlier. Confusing aspiration with overemphasis, I went too far and declared that contemplating life exclusively in its spiritual aspect could be a mutilation just as monstrous as having a disproportionate love of matter—that is, trivialization. At this point, I am better able to see the mistake in this reasoning: linked to matter through its organizing function, mind, unless it is distorted by vanity, can never be a mutilation of life.

In my moments of resistance to psychology, instead of rescuing myself from confusion by confiding in a real friend—that is, conciliatory mind—I take refuge in a false friend, an exterminator of matter which in my bewilderment I call Mind and which is no longer just one psychological function among many, but an absolute entity. I vainly identify with this Mind and become in turn the exterminator of material and sexual desires, even under their most natural and sensible forms. I dogmatize mind, and therefore also dogmatize psychology. Instead of seeing mind as a psychological function whose role is to assign values (often wrong ones), I make it into an idealized goal which will allow me to indulge my need for superiority and get my revenge by devaluing the material world, which has become all the more desirable since exterminating Mind—that is, vanity—has made it into something forbidden:

"This material world which does not accept me, this touchstone of my deficiencies—I myself will reject it as an abomination! For me it will be a symbol, the principle of Evil, Satan. I am Mind. My path is God's path."

Whenever I manage to get away with this, my pride finds its most tempting justification. I no longer belong to this world. The slightest material demands appear debasing to me. Overlain with the anguish of my inabilities, they push me back into my ivory tower, so that psychology itself, wrongly used to prop up my arrogance, becomes a prison in which, cut off from life, I feel like a corpse among the living.

These spellbinding juxtapositions of words (e.g., "mind as a function," "absolute mind") are inadequately defined and therefore contradict each other. Modern psychology is plagued with them. They are the confused result of the initial error, which vainly attempts to alternatively justify or deprecate either mind or matter. This excessive justification/accusation finally condenses into wrong ideologies of spiritualism versus materialism. Their ambivalent contradiction becomes the cause of unending quarrels of opinion, which are finally identified with the "spiritual life."[2] Mind is no longer a living and life-giving function which lies within us, the quest for essential satisfaction which can only be found in the discovery of truth; it is brought down to the level of a parlor game involving vain discussions. Indulging in these endless discussions is seen as participating in the "spiritual life." These vain discussions become a pseudo-spiritual social phenomenon and eventually exert such a strong and disruptive influence on individuals' inner deliberations that mind as the force which assigns authentic values becomes more and more bewildered and confused.

Thus, my whole fault, all my anxieties, my gnawing or even excruciating sense of despair—my "spleen,"[3] as another age would have called it—my internal discomfort, all come from attributing a wrong meaning to a word which summarizes all mental activities and psychological reflections: the word "mind."

I have just understood what it was that Diel was trying to explain to me; I can see clearly the source of my erring ways. It seems quite obvious to me. I might even be inclined to think that from now on, in situations of turmoil, I will have no trouble referring back to this vision of clarity, the source of equilibrium. . . . Wrong! Before I know it, my eyes will be veiled by affectivity. Right view will disappear, and I will once again wander about in the most obsessive state of confusion. However, while leading me into a dead end, this state will also force me to look for a way out, to ac-

[2]The French phrase *vie de l'esprit* contains an ambiguity, since it could also be translated as "intellectual life" in this context. [Translator's note]

[3]In English in the original. This term used to mean "melancholy"; it is now obsolete in this meaning in English and restricted to literary usage in French, but was quite fashionable among the *poètes maudits* of the mid-nineteenth century, especially Charles Baudelaire. [Translator's note]

knowledge ever more lucidly the basic mistake, the principle of all my agonizing distractions: the vain hypostatiza-
tion of mind. Why should I not accept this constant effort at
reasserting true values which psychology demands—which
life itself demands—and which repels me in my moments
of distraction, like the one I described earlier? Only the un-
tiring repetition of this experimental verification will
ultimately set me free, reinforcing in me a just and creative
vision.

To be effective, any creative effort must be based on
two principles: a global vision and a technique for its real-
ization. What could it be more important to apply this
creative urge to than oneself? Mind's sublimative force
manifests most authentically in the shaping of one's own
character. This genuineness can only be achieved in the
clear vision of mind's own nature, which includes the possibility of making a mistake. The essential technique for
avoiding the possible error and attaining the practical goal is
to become aware of this distorted mind, dispersed in its distorting motives, which incite one to make spurious calculations of satisfaction.

Would it be possible to become aware of unknown and
often repressed motives if there did not exist an internal law
which governs the generation of these motives and to
which the psyche is subject in its quest for satisfactions? The
relationship between vain satisfactions and the anguish of
bewilderment, the essential anguish, escapes conscious
awareness; however, the inexorability of this relationship
enables the conscious mind to discover it over and over
again. This is the crux of the method.

Reflection does in fact create a distance with regard to
the practical and immediate problems of everyday life. But
how can one possibly solve these problems without becoming detached from their emotional influence, without
resorting to elucidating and evaluating mind?

The anguish which had started to grip me after I left

Robert has just disappeared. But it may well reappear if, after withdrawing partially from Dictio, I am not able to devote my free time to the most practical activity of all: reflection and experience which reveal the laws of psychological functioning. What could be the meaning of life other than to establish mind's predominance, to prevent mind from debasing itself through mental illness in either of its two forms: exacerbated overemphasis on mind or exacerbated overemphasis on matter.

« 19 »

A Look at the Past

Despite more than thirty years of distorting life experiences, my fairly short acquaintance with psychology —which has included dealing with certain recent problems which I have outlined here—has undeniably made me feel much calmer.

In fact, all I have done so far is to extricate myself from situations. But withdrawing to a line of defense is valid only if it helps me plan a more orderly attack on the basic problems of sexuality and materiality, marriage and career.

Breaking up with Geneviève enabled me to get away from a relationship whose difficulties seemed totally unsurmountable. Contrary to my fears, I did not fall back on sexual fantasies afterward; however, my thoughts of marriage are still a bit too obsessive, although quite bearable. I also feel much more at ease at Dictio. Accepting myself as I am and assessing my situation in the company more realistically has made me much more relaxed, and the benefits of this attitude include a tolerable rapport with Robert as well as successful sales.

It is good to look back so I can tell how far I have come. I occasionally take pleasure in recalling the distant past in which I was in the depths of depression. Sometimes the contrast with the present brings back extremely painful memories, which had been buried away and almost totally forgotten. I no longer find them unbearable; instead, they take on an instructive aspect, since they show me the degree of moral decay to which false motives had led me. Take for example my breakup with my wife a long time ago. I had not really wanted to leave her. I kept sending her love letters explaining how she had made it necessary for me to break up with her, but also hoping that she would put an end to this necessity by accepting a different lifestyle. Not only was she sentimental, she was also impulsive—at heart an irresponsible and whimsical child—and it was not unlikely that the breakup might goad her into coming back. But her impulsiveness also meant that she was constantly besieged by dreams of romantic adventure, which would soon transform her acceptance into good intentions, quickly forgotten. I knew that the only way out was to be finally free of her influence. Though I missed her, in my letters I would paint a black picture of our future together to keep her from being too tempted by my hints. How terrible and fascinating were those phone calls from Italy, where I had abandoned her! We kept arranging to call each other the following day, even though we both knew it was useless to stretch out the time we were giving each other to think things over. I would wait for her call anxiously, jumping at the slightest ring when the time was getting close, afraid of not hearing the phone, afraid of going out in case she might not call at the exact time we had agreed on with such scrupulous precision. Between phone calls—in which my anguish, my sighs, and the postponed decision would make me almost speechless—I felt that my life was suspended between the impulse of love and the hate which made me write her accusing letters of complaint, letters I would never send. . . .

After my divorce, I was to feel this love-hate once again in an extremely turbulent relationship with a young woman. Though no more and no less perverted than anyone else, she nonetheless knew how to take advantage of my weaknesses and managed to drive me to the depths of despair. Whenever she thought that I had neglected her, she would reject me, and I would cling desperately. This put me totally at her mercy and made me sink into a grotesque state of complete debasement.

Stooping to obsequiousness to win her back did not move her in the least; it only made her more demanding and tyrannical. I would grovel before her, and get my revenge by debasing her through money. I no longer slept. Thin and emaciated, I was in a state of permanent nervousness—in fact, at the pinnacle of a neurosis which had started to build up since my dimly recalled childhood.

At this point I feel that no relationship with a woman will ever take me to those extremes again, because I am now able to see the degree of self-indulgence which lay hidden under the games that I took for love. In fact, I never really did take those games for love since, deep down, I knew that those women were unacceptable. It was my own self-pity, my unsatisfied need for love which I focused on them; my potential for love, but filled to the brim with self-pity. I was in love only with my heightened states, which, as my apathy grew, I tended to confuse more and more with the urge to live and the intensity of being alive.

It was the same thing in business. Many years ago, spurred by my fear of not having enough money, which had been aggravated by ill-considered expenses, I had gotten mixed up with a gambling circle. Although this went against all my principles, it held in store all kinds of promises. I found myself rubbing shoulders with the oddest assortment of people, individuals who specialized in manipulating the feverish appeal of card games. Dealers in "troubled conscience," they were the representatives of a fascinating vice, and I justified this promiscuity by being increasingly cynical at allaying my scruples. I would tell myself, for instance, that the world's corruption deserved to be attacked in its very baseness with its own weapons. Money, which I needed so much, could have no value for people willing to lose it all at the throw of a die. Tormented by the anxiety of not having enough money, I was attracted by this shady underworld, which became for a me a symbol of a dangerous lifestyle in which gains and losses come and go in an endless tide. By taking this route, which was far from the beaten paths of conventional morality, I thought that I had found a new way of embracing life completely, of overcoming my natural shyness, which actually made me tend more toward moralistic rigidity and the fear of taking risks.

Both attracted and guilty, I remained an outsider and an intruder. It was so obvious to me that I would never adapt to this world that I dared not assert my presence through a word or gesture. I felt grotesquely amorphous, tossed about, incapable of reacting—fascinated, disgusted, and scared to death. I was a far cry from the unscrupulous character which I would have liked to play, the infamous ideal which I clung to in the vain hope of overcoming my inability to take part in life, any type of life, an inability based on excessive scruples and inhibitions.

Will I ever fall into similar states of bewilderment again? At this point, it seems impossible; in fact, I can even go as far as saying it will never happen again. Having broken away from the extreme nervousness of my past, I feel, I know, that come what may, an effort similar to the one that saved me would allow me to get over any other disconcerting situation even if it took me by surprise and plunged me temporarily into despair.

These reminiscences have helped me reappraise my experience and realize how enviable my present situation is. Too inclined to forget the past, I would be wrong not to remember that at the time, I was far from hoping to achieve this relative calmness which I now feel. But perhaps my ideas about my present condition are not quite right either? It is true that the major upheavals of my past have lost their power to upset me, even though I am far from having achieved complete tranquillity. However, an indefinable dissatisfaction has taken their place, a vague melancholy that comes over me now and then. I cannot pinpoint it to any particular event—it just seems to hang like a pall over my life, sometimes for days on end. A gray feeling—no longer a roller coaster with wild ups and downs, but a veil which takes the color out of life. It is difficult to define.

It is as if deep within me there remained a lingering nostalgia for my past condition, as if I were still haunted by a feeling of restlessness. Life is no fun anymore without its ups and downs. My vanity is not satisfied with this peace, which it finds dull compared to the impetuous fantasies of bygone days. Although the only intensity which my old outbursts would bring me was that of suffering, they nevertheless allowed me to cherish mad hopes of seduction. What this means is that under the surface my heroic dreams are still smoldering, that I would still unconsciously like to surpass others rather than surpassing myself and transcending my fantasies. Having achieved harmony between my aspirations and my actions, between beauty and the obvious meaning of life, I still do not have enough vision to completely destroy my old myths.

Obviously, the humdrum routine of everyday life is not a goal in itself. Even though I may attempt to convince myself that I must try to fit in—that I must, to the extent of my abilities, serve a cause I am cut out for, no matter how modest—deep within I still nourish fanciful hopes of prestigious success, of having the cause serve me.

The idea of serving seems to involve throwing all one's strength and putting all one's interest into succeeding at a task, whether large or small, and living it with a sense of adventure, like a child at play who forgets himself. To forget my ego and its vanity means to experience with all its difficulties, yet uncomplainingly, any activity I may be involved in—instead of putting up with the situation while actually opposing it in my mind, since this turns any task into an imposition, a stereotyped duty, a wearisome bondage. Ever since my childhood, I have confused play and duty. It is this confusion which has made life colorless for me. By experiencing play in a wholesome fashion it becomes joy, since it makes one forget oneself in the present and allows one to enjoy one's body and one's capacities in full action, with no interference from any projects of prestige or vain self-consciousness, free from any anxiety or feelings of inferiority. It is wonderful to watch a child at play, putting all his heart into it, forgetting himself. A child who pretends to be a locomotive is no longer John or Jack; he becomes the locomotive and expresses it through all his gestures, oblivious of whether or not he is being watched and of grownups' indulgent smiles. A little older, he might kick a ball, have it taken away from him, get it back again. . . . The inexhaustible joy of group games, of sports. To play the game, to play at "the child running after the ball." That is the way street urchins play, and that is the way grownups should play with life's good and bad times. But that is not the way I used to play as a child, self-conscious, shy, afraid of being clumsy, afraid of looking foolish. Yet physically I was among the strongest boys in my class. Can I recall these painful memories without sinking into self-pity? In the gang of "tough guys," I was always following some leader or other who subjugated me with his arrogance. If we never beat up the weaker boys, that was because we despised them. Paying attention to them would have been lowering ourselves. Even in those days, I was already torn between admiring submission and disdainful superiority.

Can this wrong attitude be to blame for the unfortunate incident which occurred during my first contact with my schoolmates when I left the relative isolation of my home environment to be put into a boarding school? Suddenly at nine years of age, I found myself in a class swarming with children my own age, on the first day of the spring term. When my mother left me in the playground in the midst of children playing and shouting, I noticed some tears on her face; this was the first time I had ever seen her cry, and I was surprised to realize that this was possible. I was once again "outside my time," an intruder, the target and focal point for all the other boys, who knew each other since the beginning of the school year in October. One boy, a tease and a braggart, took great pleasure in pushing me around all over the place. When he tripped me up, I slammed my fist into his face and was horrified to see a large vertical scar appear in the middle of his nose, which immediately filled with blood. I made a dash for the shelter of the bathroom, followed by an avenging mob hurling insults and missiles at me over the door of the toilet. Alerted by the screams, Father Prefect came to my rescue. He gave me a talking-to for being a bully and made me stand in the corner with the other children who had misbehaved. My enemies lurked in the distance, shouting threats.

It was certainly a poor way to make acquaintances, the consequence of an attitude of submission/revolt. Under similar circumstances, a mentally more relaxed child might have seen the jostling game as great fun and jumped right in. Laughing, the boys would have quickly become friends rather than enemies.

Even at this early age, my attitude toward life was warped. I have only vague memories of my friends prior to becoming an almost permanent boarder, a situation which was to last until I graduated from Saint-Cyr. Before this, I had lived with my family. For six months I would study alone with a governess in our country home. In the winter my parents would move back to Paris and I would attend a coeducational school with my elder sisters. I probably never liked this school, since my sisters had to hold me by the hand and drag me screaming all the way. This daily scene was a real ordeal for me, and also for my sisters, who still laugh about it whenever they remember those days.

My awkwardness was a real joy for my teachers: "What is an island?" "Uhhh . . . well . . ." "Come on! You know!"

"Uhh . . . a place with . . . uhh . . . a lotta water all around . . ."

Every day we were given marks for behavior, lessons, and homework in a report card, which we had to have our parents sign in the evening. The tragedy began the day that I got straight zeros. I did not dare show my mother the report card. I got straight zeros again the next day, and again the day after. When my teacher threatened me with writing to my parents if I did not have my report card signed, I clumsily forged my mother's signature in my childish handwriting. My teacher seemed surprised. That very evening, my father demanded to see the report card. Just thinking about this fills me with terror again. I went to get the card, gave one last look at the horrible collection of zeros and the obvious forgeries . . . . I was immediately given a slap in the face and sent up to my room. A few moments later, my father came in and scolded me sharply; he told me I would end up as a swindler and a forger, dishonored and in prison. To punish me, he would send me to a boarding school. He was as good as his word—after Easter, I was transferred to the seventh grade of a boarding school outside Paris.

The world "swindler" probably rang a bell since, unable to resist the appeal of postage stamps displayed in a shop window, I had several times stolen a ten-franc note from my father's wallet, which he usually left on his night table. Two years later, in a sudden fit of religious scruples, I confessed these thefts. The penance, besides three Our Fathers and three Hail Marys, involved owning up to my father. Since I was unwilling to either admit my fault to my father or admit to the father confessor my fear of admitting, I took the initiative of atoning for my nonavowal by stepping up considerably the number of Our Fathers and Hail Marys. However, they never seemed to be enough; a moment of absent-mindedness would make me consider them ineffective and start all over again. My childish notion of self-inflicted punishment compelled me to go on forever reciting these prayers. Not knowing how to put an end to this, I once again confessed my larcenies, compounded now by my incomplete performance of the penance. After I had repeated this stratagem three or four times, the father confessor realized that there was something strange going on. He asked me to stop bothering him, assuring me that he would take any fault upon himself.

These little anecdotes, so typical of childhood, clearly show how extraordinarily afraid I was of my parents, whose behavior was apparently beyond reproach. Their mistake —a serious mistake—was to be too perfect, too strict, too moralistic, too stern, too spartan with themselves and their children. They were too exemplary. In my eyes they embodied uprightness, fairness, and honesty. Faced with these perfections, my desires became unavowable. How could they possibly have understood that I longed for those particular stamps when I had so many in my album? That those stamps were more special and more beautiful than the ones on the letters we received or the ones I would trade with my classmates?

In my child's eyes, my parents' strictness and propriety seemed like hostile rigidity because they were not compensated by any comforting warmth. Besides, warmheartedness involves understanding a child's needs instinctively, it is therefore not really in keeping with moralistic sternness. For a child, it is much more important to wear fashionable clothes and not to be the laughing stock of his classmates than to be decked out in wear-proof and stain-proof outfits responding to standards which the child, trapped in his conformity, is unable to understand. The same goes for hand-me-downs, no matter how elegant, even if they fit perfectly, especially if the child is hypersensitive and already prone to interpret things, since he would take his parents' thriftiness as a lack of consideration for him and see himself as not being worthy of anything better. Disturbed by the suspicion of not being valued, the child would look for self-esteem in his imagination, trying to establish some kind of superiority which would compensate for not feeling loved. In my case, my feeling of not being valued was even more crushing, since my parents were beyond reproach in the strict application of their principles. They had become disheartening models of an unattainable perfection, which made me consider the slightest mischief as an abominable transgression. I experienced the harrowing tension of being caught between sentimental admiration and guilty rebellion. Each time I thought of my outmoded clothes, my old toys, my lack of candles, the scarcity of visits from my friends, I would give into endless accusatory ruminations and half-repressed resentments. Although these deprivations made me feel unworthy of my parents' affection, my image of my parents was so lofty and the remorse I felt at accusing them was so strong that I could not get away from a diffuse sense of guilt which inhibited all my enthusiasm.

These reminiscences have helped me see and confirm everything that psychology has taught me. The seed of my disorder dates back to my earliest childhood. For the child, the parents' mistake becomes a trial which he must undergo successfully if the mistake and the suffering are not to be transmitted from one generation to the next.

Every individual has the possibility of cutting through this inevitable link by reviewing daily his or her distorted attitudes based on wrong motivations which are still present, although they go back to childhood. It is amazing to see how the repercussions of the mistake extend throughout a person's life, weighing ever more heavily in the mind of the adult individual, who must face greater and greater complications. It is as if the real mistake, the warped motivations which life holds every individual solely responsible for through the suffering it brings, contained in itself the need to break this disastrous chain reaction that extends over generations. Through suffering, life obliges every human being to make the effort to grow, to transform errors and mistakes into positive and satisfactory qualities. Life's cruelty does not spare us from any of the consequences of our wrong turns. As a vehicle for growth, it seems to be an essential aspect of immanent justice.

If a person were willing to deal with life's dangers in a masterly manner, the effort of sublimatory transformation would be like a joyful game: the game of mind running on the track of sane satisfactions that manifest through sane activity—like a child running after a ball just for the fun of feeling his body exerting itself, or like a horse galloping for pleasure's sake. Horses also enjoy the well-being of resting. A nervous person, however, does not know how to rest; he is always goading himself on, and his imagination is always racing toward an inaccessible activity, which, riddled with prohibitions, takes on the morbid appearance of rest—that is, toward lethargic immobility, swarming with inhibitions and shame, with the anxiety of being caught, judged, and condemned, and with the nostalgia for pretentious projects, which, through indecisiveness and stagnation, give way to despair.

Ever since my childhood, I have never enjoyed working or playing, at least not with my classmates. Before encountering psychology, I was never able to enjoy either work or play because I had never been able to create the essential conditions which would have transformed life into the play of the two complementary activities it consists of: work and restful distraction. I was always abstracted in my work and laborious in my distractions. Never integrating myself into real activity, I lived in my daydreams, away from the world.

Filled with dread at my growing incapacity, I both envied and despised those who were able to play life's game. My dread pushed me into immobility. I took refuge in my ivory tower, which was actually a tomb. Other nervous individuals attempt to escape from the dread of their isolation by releasing their nervousness outward through obsessive hyperactivity, by fleeing forward, which is just another escape tactic. Though they act out their fanciful games, reality does not meet their exorbitant expectations. Failure lies in wait for them, and each failure impels them toward new projects which are imaginatively intensified into hopes but lead only to further disappointments in a vicious circle. The further they go, the more the promises of satisfaction collapse and the emptier the successes they long for become. Perhaps they too reach the morbid and dreadful conclusion that all activities are meaningless and life itself is empty of meaning! These other nervous individuals, more or less trivialized, differ from me only in that they act out their agitation. My own nervousness always tended to lust after the secret overexcitement of the imagination. I would sink into feelings of inferiority coupled with exacerbated admiration of anybody else, whether he was of the agitated and nervous type or the trivialized type, whether he was a relatively unintelligent, trivial person capable of making level-headed decisions or an exemplary person, exceptionally gifted and able to actualize his potential fully. Putting everybody into the same bag, I raised them up on a pedestal, the better to hurl them into the depths of contempt. It is only now that I am starting to understand the nature of my illness: unable to face anything squarely—myself, other people, life's difficulties or even its joys—I never felt sure of anything. My eyes would either look up in admiration or look down with shame, but my horizon was always empty—until the day on which it slowly began to fill up.

Whether I refer to the major crises of my distant past or to my lingering feeling of apathy, I notice that my nervous temperament has not changed at all. What has improved is the character structure grafted onto it. Remembering the troubles I have overcome reinforces my hope. From a comparative perspective, it is conceivable that the lifelessness which I now feel is only the residue of my apathy. The paralyzing terror of my old anxieties has dwindled into a vague feeling of restlessness. It is forcing me to admit that my character distortion and its secret causes—that is, false justifications with regard to myself and false values assigned to the world—have not been eliminated sufficiently. Acknowledging this, I feel encouraged to persevere; evoking my past gives me hope that I may gradually go on freeing myself. The vague heaviness of heart that remains is no more than a temptation to sentimental melancholy. Nothing can free me from it if I do not persevere in my effort to correct it by assigning right values to things. By making me wholesome again, my nostalgic memories of a time of my life which I wasted irremediably will be transformed into warnings which will prevent me from repeating the same mistakes. The door to hope is wide open; all I need to do is recall these memories calmly, with neither nostalgia nor euphoria, as I am trying to do this very moment, in order for their paralyzing stranglehold to relax. My gaze has turned away from the past and is directing itself toward the healthy promises of satisfaction of the life that awaits me.

By helping me understand the events and motives of my past, introspection has turned my retrospection into projections of the future. My mind has regained its capacity to make elementary predictions. Instead of degrading itself with ruminations, it considers the future with the understanding of the past. Feasible projects take shape and become centers of interest, which is the only way to free frozen energy. My outlook is changing; a broader horizon is opening up new vistas.

« 20 »

Hopes for the Future

*I*t is late Sunday morning, and the streets are quiet and sleepy. After walking through the picturesque old streets of the downtown area, I find myself looking at detached suburban cottages. There is something touching about the childish mawkishness of their provincial conformism. I cannot be far from the train station.

I am on my way back to Paris. Yesterday, I was playing at being an administrator here. My cousins and I had come to inspect a family concern in Normandy. Details of manufacturing, management problems, personnel needs—a whole world to coordinate, which I found very interesting. Our group was jovial and cordial. Only once did I feel slightly uncomfortable, when I realized once again how little I understand of banking and legal rules, so forbiddingly complex that I admired my cousins' intellectual skill. However, the inhibition I felt at this lasted only a short while. In fact, this Saturday spent with friends in a provincial town proved to be quite pleasant.

Spring has come late this year and the weather is still cool. Looking at the houses with their closed shutters, I feel light and joyful like the morning air I am breathing. Life is beautiful! I walk slowly toward the train station, knowing that I still have plenty of time. Everything seems wonderful, and to my own surprise I start singing to myself.

Arriving at the station one hour early, I decide to wait

at the unpretentious little restaurant across the street. I need something to warm me up, because the crisp air that heralds a sunny day is starting to get to me. But no sooner do I sit down to have a coffee than I begin to worry about the time. "Just a second, miss. How much is the coffee?" One sip, and I am rushing to the station, afraid of being late though I know I am ahead of the schedule.

On the platform, I still have a good twenty-minute wait ahead of me. For the first time in my life, it feels as if the veil of my anxieties has been lifted and I am seeing the world. I am filled with delight by what I see, overcome by a strange sensation. Looking in the direction the train will be coming from, I notice that the platform and the ballast are straw-colored; the platform stretches out before me, filling the entire foreground, limited on its sides by the vertical lines of the station buildings facing each other across the tracks.

This entire landscape, a perfect composition, is transformed into a painting through the effect of the sun's rays suddenly appearing from between low clouds. The strong and intense tones of the massive shapes combine to set off the delicate grays of the details. I am moved by this beauty, in which the seldom appreciated motif of a train station is combined with the charm of a hill in the background. This awakens the painter in me, the person I once wanted to be, along with a certain attitude whose dangers I can clearly recognize. These old ambitions, which were themselves warped right from the start, are perhaps only the residue of the literary turn of mind I am struggling against. If the emotion I feel in looking at this landscape were to be infiltrated by a hint of vain admiration at my own sensitivity, supposedly exquisite and unique, the spell would be broken.

There are two or three travelers on the platform, waiting patiently like me for the morning train. The station seems to belong to an old-fashioned children's game; it reminds me of those amazing lithographs from the turn of the century. Everything is calm and immobile, and time itself seems suspended.

This contagious serenity gives my thoughts a simplicity which fills me with a sense of happiness. I cam perceive the details of nature unfolding in all its magnificent order. This vision attracts my interest, and I make an effort not to overemphasize it. At that point, the slightly excessive admiration of my surroundings gives way to a feeling of gratitude toward the experience of liberation. If this perception of the outside world arouses my interest, then the infinite aspects of inner life and the beauty of its laws should make me feel an incomparably higher, more essential, and more beneficial interest.

Here, at this moment, I feel happy. How simple things can be! I am experiencing the present, turning my attention only to the fine nuances of a landscape. But what is important is not the landscape but my inner attitude. I am focusing completely on my perceptions and thoughts, without letting my mind wander off toward the past or future. I have accepted wholesale the obligations that await me in Paris, since it is these very obligations that made me turn down my cousins' invitation to go sailing today. This distraction would have been a nice way to end a business meeting, and it did have a certain appeal compared to the obligations which are forcing me to return to Paris. I could examine them now to try to get used to them, but I would rather let my mind remain unencumbered in the present moment. My old tendency would have been to let my worries follow me onto the platform. I can just see myself: furious and complaining about having to go back, full of regret at having missed out on a chance to enjoy the vast ocean scenery. In the final analysis, events are no more than stimulants which nourish our inner life. The outside world feeds life like wood feeding a fire, like raw materials providing the basis for the existence of the factory we visited to see how we could make it operate more harmoniously. I felt a sudden interest for those activities—but is it not incomparably more interesting to find the proper setting for the "combustion" of situations which tend to upset me? Psychology has showed me that I need to look at my inner world in the same way as I am looking at this station and at this landscape. It has aroused my interest in observing the details of my experience as I go along, the moment any disturbance comes up. It has shown me how to recognize the false motives which result in inadequate psychological "combustion," leading to dissatisfaction. It has given me the means to eliminate them in order to create a harmonious vision.

Anguish has always tied me painfully to my past and future. To fully enjoy this landscape which my eyes are now resting on I must be free of cares about what was and what will be. Similarly, in contemplating my inner landscape, my anxieties are appeased by the conviction that at each present moment dissatisfaction can be dissolved through right calculations.

I realize that I am lucky to have come across this embryonic science! Its revelations would often give me a feeling of outrage, since my mind seemed to be the only one subject to the painful laws of nervous ambivalence, whereas everybody else was able to dodge them. This would bother me no end! Now that I have a tool, a weapon, it is all up to me.

A bunch of lanky schoolgirls led by a nun have just invaded the platform. What can this nun in charge of educating these girls possibly teach them about the meaning of life other than to give them ineffective and even dangerous lectures about morality? Yet, for lack of anything better, this solution seems preferable to complete disorientation. I hope that these small-town girls have enough good sense to avoid falling into excessively distorted attitudes! Behind the shutters of small provincial towns, in the apparently most peaceful villages, feelings of hate and jealousy lie smoldering. And nobody to each them the meaning of life! What comfort, what security to have a compass to guide oneself by, to have a teaching that makes finding one's bearing easier.

Easier? I am obviously experiencing a moment of euphoria. I know that soon enough I will be wrestling with my anxieties and my overexcitement. I will notice my rebellion and my suffering, without my awareness being able to cut through this troubled layer of emotionalism. But what I can be sure of, what my past experiences have shown me, is that right vision will start to gain the upper hand when I begin to elucidate the problem. All the security I have acquired rests on the certainty that I will no longer be swallowed up by emotionalism. Instead of self-indulgently prolonging the influence of emotionalism, I will cut it short and take advantage of my present feeling of composure to examine the motives which caused the disturbance and which the disturbance itself prevented me from seeing.

Like the scientist who, captivated by the marvelous laws that govern phenomena, forgets his own worries in his research, I will be able to overcome my suffering to the extent that my mind is able to grasp the inexorable causal links of the central phenomenon of our inner world, the assignment of values to motivations. This inner working of mind abides by its own laws even when applied to the aberrant calculations of vain and illusory satisfactions. It is the effects of this law which allow one to distinguish sane and insane and which finally orient one toward life's immanent meaning. Starting from the need to overcome anxiety, human beings should embark on the never-ending path which leads toward the joy of organizing all the various phenomena into a single coherent vision of truth.

But although life is made easier when one accepts the evidence of these psychological laws, the whole difficulty lies in resisting the disorderly host of desires, the pull of vain attractions, current ideologies, and popular opinions.

People are starting to move around me. My ear has just picked up the distant sound of the train. Here it comes—it has just entered this immobile landscape, ripping it apart and tearing me away from my reflections. It is heading straight for us, roaring into the station with its massive bulk and its might.

Sitting quietly in a corner of my compartment, I watch the landscape flash by with the same attitude of discovering the world which has been filling me with joy ever since this morning. Usually, no sooner would I sit down that I would bury myself in the newspaper and magazines which I had never failed to stock up on before leaving. I have often wondered about the reasons for this abnormality, a real compulsion which I had never been able to resist. It had always amazed me, yet I was unable to understand why I was not interested in a panorama which it would have been natural to enjoy, since one of the attractions of traveling lies precisely in the change of scenery. Indifferent to concrete images, to the fleeting, constantly shifting view, I was enslaved by reports on the public and private activities of other people. This stimulated my sensitivity, yet I never realized that this adulterated food robbed my mind of its substance, leaving me only a vague sense of revulsion at the bland and insipid food I had eaten. Reading was an obsession because it was a pretext to protect myself from inhibited contacts with my travel companions. It allowed me to cut myself off from the world and from my immediate surroundings. On the other hand, news items, the political and social gossip I thrived on, enabled me to keep up the illusion of contact with a world I was actually cutting myself off from. But mainly, reading was a trick to keep me from thinking, from facing myself, from listening to the question which my latent guilt was asking: "What have you done with your life? What use have you made of time fleeting by like this image of the concrete world, this landscape which you refuse to look at?"

I am filled with satisfaction, a satisfaction combining the joy of the morning sunshine and the confidence in my future which pervades my entire being. Perhaps it is this feeling of confidence which is making me discover the world and life. Could it be a sign that I am starting to free myself from the egotism which still holds me captive all too often? Yet I am sure that this momentary well-being which I am feeling is quite different from my previous passing moments of exhilaration. It is as if the sun of lucidity were shining on it. The only things in life that have value are warmth and clarity. They are the result of our having dissolved our morbid motivations, and they are also a means to achieve ever-greater freedom. I think of how much ground I have so painfully covered, yet I am also fully aware that I still have a long way to go in order for such states of wakefulness to become the habitual fabric of my life, without too many hitches.

Postscript

More than ten years have gone by since I wrote the numerous notebooks from which the preceding sections have been excerpted. At the time, I was endeavoring to elucidate my subconscious motives between therapy sessions in order to fight against their disastrous influence on my behavior. This practice sharpened my analytic faculties, and I have long since achieved an autonomy which allows me to do without analytic help. Besides, I no longer live in Paris. I see Diel only two or three times a year. I feel free not only of individual neurotic symptoms, but of the agonizing bewilderment which underlies all symptoms of nervous over-excitement or inhibition.

I owe Diel my joy in being alive. The least I can do in return is to help him propagate the ideas which gave me this sense of joy. This is why I offered him my notebooks so that he could use them to illustrate his method. This decision came to me quite recently as I was rereading my journals. More than ever before, I became aware of the radical change which has come about in my existence. From its very beginning, analysis divided my life into a *before* and an *after.* I am no longer assailed by the abulic hesitations and the resistance to therapy which these journals bear witness to. They have given way to confidence in the practical truthfulness of this teaching that I was able to benefit from. This is not to say that I now live in a state of imperturbable satisfaction.

The wounds have healed, but the scars are still sensitive sometimes.

I am obviously still a nervous person—or rather a person of nervous temperament—and I always will be. The subconscious—the tendency to imaginative overexcitement and the different types of blindness which result from it—can never be definitely overcome. However, thanks to the continuous practice of autonomous self-analysis, temptations to backslide quickly trigger off an alarm whose responsiveness has grown in proportion to my increasing ability to detect lapses. The sky of my life may not always be perfectly blue, but no dense fog will ever obscure my view again, nor will storm clouds ever again get a chance to build up dangerously.

This self-assurance is due to the irreversibility of psychological experience. Anyone who has seen his anguish dissolve and felt hope open up before him will never again fall prey to any form of despair for very long, for the increasing intensity of his suffering will sound off a warning, rousing him to once again make the effort to attain the hope he had glimpsed. It is suffering that makes one look for the perverted motivations behind a relapse and forces one to consider one's despair in terms of the laws that govern it, rather than submitting passively to it and wallowing in self-pity. This method of working on myself has given me not only self-confidence but also joy: the assurance that no disaster can ever cause me permanent harm, since the beneficial force of analysis allows one to turn misfortune into good fortune by either transforming the situation or accepting its inevitable aspects.

I am far from claiming that my joy is imperturbable. Contrary to what I used to believe, joy is not a permanent state of mind but a vital dynamic energy which will always be able to restore the necessary degree of cheerfulness and warm-heartedness.

I now live in the country, far from Paris. I have been

married for five years and have a four-year-old son. Reducing my needs and adjusting them to my fortune has enabled me to temporarily abandon the idea of practicing a profession. I know how enviable this material privilege is and how it can give rise to resentments over my condition. But it seems to me that very few people could have been able to adapt to an existence as lacking in habitual distractions as the one I have chosen.

Work and marriage can both induce one to adopt a middle-class outlook, either by giving rise to excessive resentments or by deadening one's spirit through submission to conventions and the humdrum routine of habits. Family life with its dangers gives me ample occasion for observing myself and correcting my behavior. Describing and reflecting on these dangers in writing has become an indispensable and joyful occupation, to which I devote a considerable part of my day. All I ask of myself in my present married condition is to be able to create, and especially to maintain, an atmosphere of warmth conducive to harmonious relations with my wife and favorable to the education of my son. The best way, then, to present my state of mind and my occupations in this postscript is to write about the conditions of my married life and my efforts to overcome my difficulties with the help of my psychological knowledge.

Therapy improved my condition to the point of freeing me from the exacerbated fears and hopes which I had attached to the idea of marriage, thus putting me in the position of being able to grasp the opportunities presented to me in terms of their real possibilities and to eventually meet the woman I am now married to. Marrying her was one of the most decisive choices I have ever made. My improved condition also made it possible for a level-headed woman of good sense to choose to marry me and consent to share with me the solitary existence which we lead. But what would be the point of having learned to choose if I were not able to trust my choice, to be true to my choice and to myself, true to the force of my trust in our joint life and my commitment[1] to it. Marriage would be a prison if I were not able to constantly fall in love with my wife all over again, if I did not continually choose to renew my commitment to her. This points at the importance not only of making the right choice but also, as psychology suggests, of making the daily effort to dissolve resentful ruminations and escapist fantasies. Only such an effort can give marriage its deepest meaning by preventing one from adopting a middle-class outlook.

This is the flame of psychological insight which has given my hearth all its warmth and gentleness. I must naturally give credit to my wife, since her intuitive good sense often comes to my rescue when my nervous temperament occasionally makes me ill-humored. Despite the link we have established between the best in ourselves, our weaknesses can be cause for quarrels, as with all couples. But our disagreements are never prolonged into ruminations and rancor. I am too aware that the worst thing one can do is to project blame exclusively on the other, but also that it would be just as inadequate for me to take on half the blame out of pseudo-generosity. In varying degrees of intensity, we each carry the entire fault within ourselves: the tendency toward false motivations. This is doubtless one of psychology's most beneficial discoveries. All I need to do is to remind myself of this to be able to smile again and feel a sense of warmth, and my wife immediately responds to this. I see

[1]This sentence and the following one hinge on an untranslateable play on words. The French word which I have translated here as "commitment" is *fiance*, a nonexistent back-formation from the word *fiancée*. *Fiancée* is the past participle of the verb *fiancer*, "to betroth," and its reflexive form *se fiancer*, "to become engaged," and is etymologically related to the verb *se fier*, "to trust," the noun *confiance*, "trust, confidence," and the adjective *fidèle*, "true, faithful." Similarly, the archaic English expression "to plight one's troth" means "to pledge one's truth," i.e., to make a commitment; "betrothal" (*fiançailles*) refers to a mutual pledge to marry, an engagement, a commitment; and the words "truth" and "trust" are etymologically related. [Translator's note]

her face light up without a shadow of resentment. This enables me to avoid untimely psychological explanations, which would only aggravate the quarrel. Seldom does one meet a person who is willing to forgo the satisfaction of replying to a gesture of reconciliation with either sulkiness or a triumphant attitude. It would be wrong for me to deny that she is a true lesson in innate wisdom.

In turn, I educate her by helping her go beyond the limits of good sense and recognize the overriding helpfulness of psychological knowledge. In spite of her levelheadedness, she is often disconcerted by some of our son's reactions to the first constraints of socialization.

With her receptive wisdom, my wife accepts and assimilates very well any explanation I might be willing to give her at a timely moment, and this reinforces our harmony considerably. Our mutual appreciation grows day by day. She is able to communicate with me on the level of ideas. I am happy to see that she shares the life of my mind instead of refusing to have anything to do with it on the pretext that it is too theoretical or that I often neglect her by shutting myself up in my room to write. This gives her a practical understanding of psychology, which she skillfully applies in the education of our son.

As for our son, he is like a photographic developer who reveals his parents' mistakes. He demands that adults be warm and lucid, patient and thoughtful, that they overcome their wrong motivations. Educating our child stimulates and amplifies our mutual educational process. My wife and I never fail to observe that whenever our son gets obstinate it is because our actions were either dogmatic impositions or conventional reflexes. Even though an indispensable part of a child's education involves teaching him to adjust to the customs and habits of the social environment he is destined to inhabit, the most essential aspect of all is making sure that the cause of all his morbid dissatisfactions—the innate false motivations which are latent in him—does not develop excessively.

Adult conventions are meaningless to a child. When these conventions are imposed on him, all this means to him is that his primitive desires, which demand immediate satisfaction, are being restrained. But even stronger than the primary demands of his desires is his essential need to rest in his parents' esteem and to be guided by their love and understanding—the only things that will get him to accept undesired conventional impositions. This possibility for a just solution exists, and is in fact inscribed in the child's very nature; therefore, if parents refuse to be both firm and fair in getting the child to do what he will willingly do in exchange for their love and understanding, he will quite predictably see this as the most essential injustice of all. This refusal deprives the child of an essential joy. Excessive attempts to impose conventions or excessively sentimental love which gives way too easily to the child's apparent obstinateness will both be perceived by him as a deprivation of an essential need, as an aggressive injustice which will slowly awaken his own innate tendency to make false justifications.

The crucial and most difficult problem of a child's socialization is achieving the proper balance between adjustment to social norms and education of his essential nature.

If I dwell on this difficulty in these pages, this is not from a desire to talk about theory (although I disagree with the most current educational theory, which states that the ultimate aim of a child's education is to adjust the child to the rules of the game dictated by society). I have not forgotten the purpose of this postscript, which was to talk about my present life. But this particular situation actually happens to be the most concrete issue in my life at this point. Faced with this difficult task, I occasionally become impatient, as does my wife. But psychological knowledge implies foresight. I know exactly what would happen if, instead of protecting myself from the danger of impatience and resentments, I were to give in to them.

I shudder at the thought of the inextricable situation of "fatherhood" into which I would have strayed if I had not read the book which deals specifically with the issue of motivations in educational situations.[2] I went into this more thoroughly during my analysis, extracting from it the guiding principles which are helping me avoid the mistakes I suffered from during my own childhood. Taken by surprise, I would have no doubt acted in accordance with conventions. I would have played the role of the learned sage who knows nothing of what he teaches and who teaches false truths, truths which are unteachable because they are unintelligible to the child. I would have demanded that the child take my word at face value and would have repressed any objections; or else I would have fallen into the opposite mistake, thoughtlessly giving in each time, afraid that the child might respond with excessive resistance, leading to complexes.

All my childhood and youth were spent under the influence of a network of conventional inhibitions so overwhelming that their stranglehold crushed my spirit, making me into a spineless human being and ruining my spiritual appetite.

"Why?"—this is the child's endless question. "Because it's good for you, and the reason it's good is because I say so and because everybody else says so!" This is complete disregard to the child's essential need, which is sacrificed to conventional adaptive socialization. The growing child's repressed questions are transformed into accusatory criticism of his parents and finally of society. My illness was no more than a repressed question, which I was never given an answer to. Therapy cured me by giving my questions a satisfactory answer, thus freeing me from the profound feeling

[2]See Paul Diel, *The Psychology of Re-education* (Boston: Shambhala Publications, 1987).

of not being valued, which became guilty self-contempt in the face of society's conventional impositions.

Is it possible that I in turn may not have sufficient regard to my child's needs? Each time the bond of affection and esteem between my child and myself is disturbed, I notice that he begins to wall himself off in his own self-esteem, which, blown up into vain self-conceit, manifests as capricious disobedience. This has forced me to realize that it is up to me to come to his aid by transforming my sullen attitude into understanding and openness, showing him that he has by no means lost my esteem for good. This is really what children, in their sensitivity, are most afraid of, and are only able to express at this age through the revenge of their obstinate disobedience. Whenever I understand this, my voice and my face immediately change and express friendliness again. It is amazing and heartwarming to see how eagerly my young son—too healthy to sulk for any length of time—responds to the esteem I offer him by instantly dropping his attitude of vain self-conceit and once again presenting his parents with the gift of obedient trust.

It would be impossible for me to have noticed this if I had never heard about the notion of calculating one's satisfaction and the vain distortions to which this calculation is prone. The educational relationship is an opportunity to observe how the various shades of self-justification and disobedient escapism are born, already tainted with guilt, though not yet transformed into habitual character distortions. I am always surprised to see the precision with which analytic understanding enables me to sweep away the imponderable dust of resentments and in so doing discover the only effective form of action.

Repeating this beneficial experience creates resonances of long duration both in the child and his parents, and the inevitable educational mistakes which one makes now and then remain isolated problems without repercussions—for the very reason that past disappointments were not able to build up into a sediment of resentment or a wall of resistance. It is touching to see my son graciously grant me the right to be wrong sometimes.

Eventually my son will be old enough so that I can address his reason directly. What a joy to feel absolutely certain that I will be able to teach him the exact meaning of all the virtues and qualities that children never stop hearing about: beauty, goodness, courage, intelligence, truthfulness. How can I help but feel joyful at the prospect of explaining to my son one day that these qualities are linked together through a law, a form of justice, life's immanent justice; that they can be ruined only through the assault of all the wrong justifications summarized in the word "vanity"—or in the expression "repressed guilt," which is another way of saying the same thing; and that vanity carries within itself its own punishment, which is the supreme manifestation of immanent justice.

In speaking about my son's education, I am only repeating the teaching and the experience which enabled me to reeducate myself. I am only transmitting to him the spiritual legacy I have received. Could my son reject it, any more than I myself rejected it? "The vital satisfaction that we are all looking for is subject to conditions which can be understood through understanding its laws." Since my son has been experiencing this law since his earliest childhood, and will later have it explained to him in precise terms at an age when his receptiveness will be opening up to ideas which will impress it forever, the path will be open for him. He will be able to avoid countless mistakes. My own effort will be his opportunity. His joy will be proportionate to his receptivity, his spirit, his appetite for truth.

Thus I will not only have lived for myself. The result of my so-called egoism, which compelled me to take the necessary steps to cure myself, will be, I hope, the possibility of a successful life for my son, whom I will try to protect as best I can against the assaults of the mistakes and erring ways which caused me so much suffering.

Analyst's Epilogue

It would be impossible for this diary of a psychoanalysis to be the complete reflection of a therapeutic approach. As a fragmentary illustration, it can help pose the problem of the possibility of an introspective method, but it cannot guarantee this method against every possible objection.

The case presented here is exceptional both in terms of the patient's privileged social situation and of his spirit of perseverance in deep self-examination. It therefore runs the risk of having all attacks focus on it. But it also presents an advantage which is essential to the introspective method, discredited as egocentric and antisocial: the obligation to analyze thoroughly the relationship between an individual and the demands of social life.

I will not reexamine here the therapeutic approach, illustrated in a more or less representative manner throughout the patient's journals. But I will, by way of conclusion, add a few explanations which seem indispensable.

Proponents of analytic theories which aim at adjusting the individual to the norms of social life will be predictably unanimous in objecting that the outcome of the therapy—withdrawal from professional life—was just an "easy way out" and that offering the nervous individual the escape of shutting himself in a sort of extended ivory tower, restricted to his family life, does not amount to curing him.

I am perfectly ready to admit that a livelihood is not

only desirable but in most cases a prerequisite, if not for a cure, then at least for the improvement of an individual's mental health. Idleness is dangerous because it favors the appearance and development of escapist and justificatory fantasies. Earning a living allows one to ensure one's material basis, and this can allay the imaginary accusations which the nervous person is prone to direct against society. But the opposite can also be true, and the obligation of having to practice a profession considered to be insufficiently well paid or prestigious can lead to an excess of morbid ruminations.

In more general terms, one can observe that the practice of a profession only gives rise to balanced satisfaction, which in turn fosters greater balance if it goes hand in hand with the full development of a very important quality, conscientiousness.[1] This quality, however, is often threatened by two risks of perversion. The first, harmful to society, is unscrupulous social climbing, which sees work only as an opportunity for acquiring wealth and power; the second risk, harmful mainly to the individual, is the excessive idealization of work, which is seen as a mission to be accomplished. Thus, work itself can become the cause for pathogenesis, a crushingly overemphasized task which collapses in an excess of inhibitive scruples because of the person's excessively good intentions. (I will mention only one example, that of a doctor racked by endless scruples each time he had to make out a prescription, for fear of making a mistake which could be fatal to the patient and harmful to his own career. In varying degrees, this deformation of conscientiousness is quite frequent among professionals who must take on human responsibilities, such as doctors and teachers.)

One might object that these flagrant cases of professional maladjustment in no way disprove the theory which

[1]The word for "conscientiousness" in French is *conscience professionnelle*, which carries associations not only with *conscience* and *consciousness*, but also with *profession*. (Translator's note)

sees adjustment to one's work as a therapeutic principle. This is to forget that making one's work into one's reason for living gives rise to a form of "illness of the conscience,"[2] since it makes people into trivial, success-oriented go-getters. Although this is generally considered a very healthy and fairly satisfactory form of adjustment, trivial over-valuing of one's work is only a form of idealistic wrong justification. The only way to cure this is to dissolve the underlying false motivations.

Thus, one is led to admit that the healing principle lies not in being gainfully employed, that is, in participating in the production of material goods, but in dissolving resentments of superiority and inferiority, whether these feelings manifest at work or outside it. This is far from being an "easy way out," for either the patient or the analyst.

If the patient has in fact been progressively cured of his resentments, then the withdrawal for which he is being criticized is in no way a retreat into an ivory tower but, on the contrary, an openness of mind which actually enables him to frequent his acquaintances and relations in all friendliness, no matter what their opinions or judgments about him may be.

Perhaps one should avoid using images like "ivory tower" in a stereotyped fashion. If one really thinks about it, the image applies only in reference to a specific psychological condition. Instead of being content with vague allusion through image, it might be better to clearly define the image's hidden meaning, which can be identified only because it belongs to the sphere of inner motivations which determine our social actions and interactions. In terms of motivations, the only possible meaning of the expression "ivory tower" is "escape into egocentric ruminations" caused by a vanity which longs to triumph but is continually assailed by feelings of inferiority, guilt-ridden at its

[2]The French word *conscience* can mean both "conscience" and "consciousness." [Translator's note]

excessive dependence on others' opinions, imagined to be unsympathetic and hostile, and caught up in never-ending ruminative counterattacks, emotional accusations directed against others and the world.

The patient's condition improved to the extent that analysis managed to undo the apparently inextricable knot of resentments. The patient will continue to progress toward a cure to the extent that he manages to further free himself from the anguish of being condemned by prevalent ideologies, the strongest of which are two fundamental mistakes pregnant with complex consequences: that the point of being a human being is either to practice a material profession or to indulge in sexual debauchery.

The author of these journals considered himself a *déclassé*, someone who has gone down in the world. Submitting to society's demands in order to escape from his overwhelming feelings of inferiority, he ended up choosing one of the most absurd paths: he decided to finance a tiny business concern with no real chances of success in the hope of being able to play at being the boss, only to end up playing the servant's role because of his lack of skills.

Should I have encouraged him to persevere in such nonsense? To start one such business after the other until his pecuniary resources were depleted? Or should I perhaps have advised him to accept a junior position in a large corporation to prevent him from squandering his money? It is useless to evoke all the humiliations to which he would have been exposed and which might very well have exacerbated his resentments and aggravated his condition.

I could of course have told him that he should just put up with a situation which is a consequence of his previous mistakes, thus proving that he is redeemable—and if not, too bad for him. Obviously, anyone is entitled to say this except, perhaps, the therapist—unless the therapist is convinced that there is nothing more essential or important for one's mental health than having a livelihood. Should the therapy fail, this will enable him to tell his client: "I did everything I could for you. Unfortunately, you just happen to be one of those cases—quite common, actually—which are refractory to adjustment and cannot be cured." This is both to condemn the patient and to justify a curative method based exclusively on adjustment to the habitual demands of one's social environment. Can it be right to condemn a person who is placing his last hopes in the therapy, thus sentencing him to a collapse into dejection which may very well be final?

Seeing no possibility of helping the patient to adjust in a way which would be satisfactory both for him and for society to a commercial career which he had haplessly chosen for a number of wrong reasons, I therefore undertook to disengage him from an imperative which had become obsessive and crushing. I was all the more convinced that it was necessary to free him from this absurd experience, since not only had it lasted long enough to be conclusive, but also perfectly legitimate doubts had started to come up.

To demand, no matter what, that the patient achieve an impossible satisfactory adjustment would have been the most serious mistake that one could commit in analyzing the social situation, which necessarily goes hand in hand with the analysis of inner motivations. The patient's remaining good sense would no doubt have warned him confusedly that he can actually live without earning a living and that it is unfair to oblige him to do so at all costs. His resistance to the real injustice of both the therapy and the therapist would have been the cause for the final failure of the analysis.

As I had turned my patient away from his business career, and even from the idea of having to look for a solution in this area given his lack of inclination and skills, there was only one way to integrate him into the sphere of work: to have him acquire the university degrees necessary to practice one of the liberal professions. One can imagine the number of difficulties that he would have had to overcome. I will only mention his age and the fact that his intelligence was not of the scholarly type. Aroused in the course of the analysis, his intelligence manifested as an increasing interest in the teachings of introspective psychology. These teachings do not oppose the practice of any profession; on the contrary, they can make work easier for individuals who are overwhelmed by ruminative resentments. By dissolving these resentments, they can free time and energy, which then become available for sane activities. However, analysis can only play this facilitative role if it opposes the over-valuation of work, which often makes it obsessive and crushing.

In this particular case, the insight the patient had gained through analysis could hardly have induced him to go back to school determined to cope with the difficulties of uncertain academic success. I feel entirely or at least largely responsible for guiding the patient away from this path leading toward the practice of a profession. This compels me to take upon myself any criticism that might be formulated.

Any criticisms that might subsist after this clear explanation of the case would, I think, boil down to this: "He should just be like everybody else." And since "being" here actually refers to behavior, which depends on the value judgments one has secretly made in one's own mind, the criticisms can be summarized in the following lapidary formula: "He should just think like everybody else." And he should—as long as what everybody else thinks is the truth! This puts the problem in a nutshell.

Considering the persistent criticism directed against the analyst and his method, I would like to conclude by briefly presenting the reasons which lead me to think that adjusting to society as it is defined by modern thought can-not possibly enable individuals to realize life's essential value, the only principle which can actually heal mental illnesses.

It might be helpful to point out in passing that I have no intention of coming up with new arguments here to defend my cause. All my previous publications were designed to show that guiding values are not transcendental in origin, nor is their origin social in the usual sense of the word, but that they are biologically immanent, implicit in the conditions of our existence, and that it is up to psychology to make them explicit by bringing together all of life's aspects: preconscious, conscious, supraconscious, and subconscious.

I will therefore use this diary as an illustration to highlight a new aspect of this initial proposition, an aspect which I feel to be especially helpful in underscoring the importance—the necessity, even—of an in-depth analysis of the relationship between individuals and society. The correction proposed—if developing one's initial proposition can be terms a correction—can only be done through an in-depth examination of the problem. Far from being a sidetrack, this examination is actually the most direct way to extricate oneself from confusion, in this case as in any other case.

All cultures of the past, and even our culture, were originally based on a supraconscious vision of the meaning of life as expressed through the collective dreams of myths. Mythologies, whether pagan or monotheistic, would be unable to forge the cultural unity of a people if they did not contain the vision of guiding values, sublimatory action motives disguised symbolically and personified as divinities. By denying the predominance of this cultural need, attested historically through the existence of mythologies, and regarding the life of communities as based purely on common material needs, one misjudges the real depth of the social issue.

The life of societies has two aspects: the culture of a

people and their civilization. Culture seeks adjustment to the meaning of life; civilization deals with adjustment to the environment. Civilizing adaptativeness is fully justified as long as it does not lose sight of the predominant necessity of adjusting to the meaning of life. When this essential vision is lost, the culture declines since social life begins to overflow with unbridled material demands.

Since it is not possible to elaborate in great detail the cultural and essential aspect of the social problem, I will refer the reader to previous publications which attempt to decipher the hidden meaning of mythic symbolism and to show that myths contain psychological foreknowledge. In describing in enigmatic language the combat between gods and demons, heroes and monsters, myths are actually speaking of the conflicts of the human soul and pointing to valid and invalid solutions. In addition, myths contain the "biogenetic basis for man's conflicting situation."[3]

When mythical images are taken at face value because a society ceases to understand their symbolic language, their explanatory power is diminished and doubt starts to gnaw away at the inadequate explanation. The supraconscious vision of guiding values loses its unifying force and breaks down into a multitude of contradictory ideologies, which can be classified into two groups: spiritualist dogmas and materialist dogmas.

At this point, adjusting individuals to society no longer involves leading them toward sociability through the unifying vision of values, but merely adjusting them to contradictory ideologies, to collective action motives. Culture in turn degenerates into bookish knowledge that enables "cultured" people to discuss and even quibble about the different ideologies offered, so as to be in a position to be able to take a stand one way or the other.

[3]Paul Diel, *Symbolism in Greek Mythology* (Boulder: Shambhala Publications, 1980); *La Divinité: Etude psychanalytique* (Paris: P.U.F., 1949); *The God-Symbol* (New York: Harper & Row, 1985).

An ideology is a collection of ideas based on assigning right or wrong values. Since life can only have one meaning, valid for all living beings, there should be only one ideology, valid for all human beings and for all human activities. The term "meaning" contains two complementary elements: direction and value. Sane direction can only be directed to evolutionary growth; ethical value is the spirit that drives individuals toward this growth. As long as multiple ideologies continue to exist, the should at least possess common roots in profound biological truth to unify them; otherwise, they will always remain, at least in part, wrong directions— involuntionary, erroneous, and unwholesome.

For human beings, profound biological truth can be defined in terms of the adaptive process which rules evolution. Unlike animals, humans not only adapt to their environment, but have also learned to adapt the environment to their appetites and material comfort, which have diversified into countless desires. However, the evolutionary demand which is valid for everyone is still there; it is the biogenetic law that states that the unity of common origin must not be lost, in spite of differentiation.[4] Since unity in multiplicity amounts to harmony, this evolutionary law compels human beings to harmonize their desires, which they can do only on the level of inner deliberations.

The excessive and disharmonious multiplication of sexual and material appetites is a mistake of value-assigning mind. It is both biologically harmful and psychologically pathogenic, in that it can go far beyond both organic need (the need of the psychosomatic organism) and the environmental conditions for its satisfaction. The biopsychological law that governs human life stipulates that the disharmonious overemphasis on appetites results in their anguished inhibition, since, in the final analysis, exacerbated desires cut themselves off from the very conditions for their sane satisfaction. Wrong valuations break up the harmony of

[4]Paul Diel, *Fear and Anguish* (Claremont, Calif.: Hunter House).

values into ambivalences. No ideological justification of the exacerbation of sexual or material desires can in the long run ward off inhibiting anxiety and guilt. The biopsychological law which governs human life is an ethical law; it is not an ideology invented by man, and it will not obey any ideology that man could ever invent.

Mythical symbolism expresses with great precision both aspects of this immanent ethical imperative: on the one hand, the need for the full and harmonious development of desires, a prerequisite for their essential satisfaction; on the other, the punishment of their exacerbation through pathos, through the pathological inhibition of spiritual, material, and sexual desires, which gradually become impotent. In symbolic language, punishment and reward are imposed by judge-deities, which represent the immanent requirement for harmony. Pathologically exacerbated appetites are symbolized by devouring monsters, whereas demons represent unwholesome mind, degraded into the false justifier of exacerbation.[5]

This leads to the hope that immutable ethical truth may gradually be formulated not only in supraconscious and symbolic terms, but also conceptually, consciously, knowingly. The so-called exact sciences—especially its prototype, physics, with its technical ingenuity—which give us mastery over our environment, will find their indispensable complement, the science of life and its curative technique giving us gradual mastery over ourselves.

The essential point of human life is to understand the immanent ethical law in order to be able to overcome accidental ideological overvaluations or undervaluations of material and sexual appetites. This is the real function of mind. It is only through applying this function that mind can exert its curative power.

Excessive overvaluation of work necessarily results in a backlash, that is, the excessive undervaluation of work,

[5]See *Symbolism in Greek Mythology*.

which sees any material preoccupation purely as a sign of a middle-class mentality. This leads, on the level of secret motivations and later on the level of behavior, to the complementary mistake which reacts against unleashed materiality with unleashed sexuality, itself overvalued as a magnificent adventure, the means to escape from the drudgery of work.

There can be no doubt that materiality and sexuality are basic values since they are indispensable for the maintenance of life. However, it must be made clear—and this clarification is the aim of any in-depth examination—that the healthy maintenance of life depends on the right estimation of these basic values, the only way to establish a hierarchy of values.

All the motivating conditions, value-assigning spirituality as well as materiality and sexuality, are implied in the problem of therapeutic psychology, which thus poses the complete problem of life. Thus stated, the central issue of therapy is to prevent the biological implication of all situations of existence from becoming a tangle of confusions because of wrong valuations. In the final analysis, it may well be that this tangle of confusions is the consequence of our common overvaluation of professional success.

Under the pretext of sociability, material ambition transforms everyone's social life and individual psychology into a veritable jungle of resentments of superiority and inferiority. The fierceness of this struggle absorbs everyone's energies. From childhood, people are oriented toward getting a degree which will enable them to earn their living, and nobody has any time or desire any more to reflect on the essential problem of life. Besides, because of the excessive specialization of work, people would not be able to do it even if they wanted to.

Thus, it is society that is in fact shutting itself off in an ivory tower of collective euphoria which excludes any true reference to the psychological under the pretext that everything is just fine this way. On the contrary, things are far from being just fine, as everybody is starting to realize.

To make individuals accept the idea of material work, the foundation of collective existence, society proposes ideologies along the following lines: "The individual is no more than the product of society"; "Society is more than the sum of its individuals"; "Individual behavior is totally determined by social influence"; or "Psychological functioning is just a negligible epiphenomenon." All this would be true if the individual were no more than a cog in the social wheel. It is false to the extent that the individual is capable of inner deliberation, since this unceasing deliberation is in fact constant introspection aimed at elaborating personal action motives.

This statement might seem patently obvious. Nothing, however, would be less superfluous than to repeat it ad nauseam. People have great difficulty understanding it because it goes against all of their preconceptions. Its innumerable consequences can only be identified through in-depth analysis, which opens the way to a whole universe of ideas radically opposed to ideological prejudice, as well as to superstitions and dogmas.

The proof of the pathogenic influence of most of the prevalent ideologies lies in their ambivalence, since they all put forward two contradictory scales of values which are cause for bewilderment; they oscillate between spiritualism and materialism, exacerbated idealism and trivial ambitiousness, moralism and amorality, altruism and egoism.

It follows that there are two ambivalent forms of mental illness: nervòusness and trivialization. One is the consequence of anguished bewilderment, the other of euphoric conventionalization. Trivialization is not usually diagnosed as mental illness; on the contrary, it is considered an ideal adjustment to society, a state of being cured from nervousness. Actually, the entire issue of a healthy or unhealthy relationship between individuals and society is condensed in the notion of trivialization. Trivialization is a mental illness not only because it involves the conventionalization of mind; it is unhealthy because it is lopsided, because it overvalues and exacerbates material and sexual appetites to the detriment of mind.

Its false ideal is exhibition without scruple. This makes individuals feel euphoric, giving them a false feeling of liberation. Trivial exacerbation tries to free itself from the fundamental law that stipulates that every exacerbation is followed by inhibition. The attempt is in vain, since unscrupulous overemphasis on materiality and sexuality can only be obtained through inhibition of the mind and its appeal to achieve harmony. The false value judgments which result in trivialization unite people on a socially uneven level. The absence of scruples in relations between individuals destroys sociability and is the main cause for hateful resentments. Shameless euphoric exhibition becomes the scourge which strikes at the heart of societies—unlike nervousness, which strikes only at the heart of the individual.

The apparently theoretical pages of this diary are landmarks for the different stages of the cure. Through an in-depth exploration, the author attempts to identify the false motives that make him support current ideologies and adhere to their contradictory value judgments, resulting in a sense of disorientation and anguished split. By understanding the pathogenic influence of false promises of satisfaction justified through ideologies—false and pathogenic because they lead alternatively to exacerbation and inhibition—it is possible to free oneself from the resistance against therapeutic experience and its teaching and to progress toward the unification of one's own judgment.

The unification of one's value judgments is a curative principle for societies too. Sociability can only be established to the extent that individuals share a common vision of guiding values. From the integrity of their values results sane integrity of individuals' characters. Having an integral vision of values shapes character, since it dissolves exacerbated ambivalences leading to falsely motivating resentments, which are in turn the cause for antisocial interactions. It would obviously be pleasant to live in a social environment where, by educational transmission from one generation to the next, all individuals had become capable of more or less lucid introspection allowing them to dissolve resentments for their own good and the good of the community. One wonders whether this is not the real solution to the social problem.

Obviously, societies evolve at a slower rate than individuals, who can achieve relative wholesomeness in the course of their ephemeral lifespans. Individuals who, goaded on by either suffering or enthusiasm, decide to undertake the effort to achieve liberation by themselves will have to bear in mind that their social milieu will evolve very slowly if they are to keep themselves from falling back to the self-indulgent resentments of people who feel "misunderstood."

If the author of this diary, through his daily practice of questioning the value of unwholesome motivations, was able to gradually liberate himself from his guilty vanity and thus transform it into a modest pride at his relative accomplishment, I dare say that he has done more for his own cure and for the evolutionary hope of society as a whole than if he had stuck to practicing any profession or adhered to any of the prevalent ideologies. They are all based in fact on phobic ignorance of our unceasing introspective deliberation, which thus becomes morbid because it is insufficiently controlled, and also on ignorance of the extraconscious mind, whether in its ancestral form—the mythical dreams of societies—or in its present form—daydreams and nightdreams. In fact, the most dangerous daydreams are today's prevalent ideologies, be they pseudo-spiritual, material, or sexual.

	DATE DUE		